A Really Huge CHRISTMAS CAROL, Believe Me

Don't Mourn, Satirize

ALEC PRUCHNICKI

PREFACE

B oth—the climate of this season and the events in current political affairs—tend to send a shiver up our spines. May I humbly add a modest ghost story to this list to entertain and illuminate our thoughts. May readers enjoy this in the spirit in which it is written.

CHAPTER ONE

F red Trump was dead, to begin with. There is no doubt whatever about that. Not only had it been a blow, though expected, to his family, but it was announced in numerous newspapers and television reports. Each gave an account, whether brief or detailed, of his numerous accomplishments and equally numerous scandals and controversies. He left his fortune to his family, at least to most of his family, and he passed on the love of real estate mostly to his son Donald. It is on Donald that this story centers, although numerous others, alive and dead, would be involved. This is a ghost story, after all.

The details of Donald's rise from a second-born son to master of real estate have been discussed elsewhere, because of his prominence. I will only touch on them as they contribute to this story, which begins many years after Fred's death when Donald has achieved the ultimate accomplishment. He has just been elected President of the United States. By both skill and luck, bluster and bravado, and numerous lies and libels, he has surpassed his father's, and possibly his own, wildest dreams. But this is not the final climax of our story, it is only the beginning.

Donald sat alone in his massive apartment in his modestly named Trump Tower in the heart of New York City. He thought back to his days in Brooklyn when he would glimpse the towers of the city (as borough residents referred to Manhattan) with much of the same thrill as Dorothy when glimpsing the spires of the Emerald City, or as fellow Brooklynite Tony Manero felt in *Saturday Night Fever*. There was wealth, and power, and especially fame for the taking. A second-born son of a nouveau riche family in a relatively quiet corner of greater New York could conquer the world if he could conquer Manhattan. At what point he desired to do this, and at what point he actually believed he could do this, isn't clear. But the details of his growth would have to wait for his memoirs many years later. Now he faced more difficult problems.

It was Christmas Eve. This was the last one he would celebrate as a private citizen, and already the duties of his impending position were starting to weigh on him. He knew that as president every action he would take would be examined under a figurative microscope by enemies and even envious friends. He only had a few weeks during this hectic Christmas season to tidy up as many business deals as possible before handing them over to his children, who would, in turn, be scrutinized for their ethical behavior. These enterprises, both honest and shady, had to be as clean as possible to protect his kids.

He sat behind his oversized and untidy desk, with his Secret Service protectors instructed to stay in the next room, and looked over his last-minute schedule. His wife and children had all accepted President Obama's invitation to come and spend Christmas Eve in the White House, in a spirit of reconciliation and transition. Donald stayed behind temporarily and was to meet them there after he finished his business appointments, but he was running very late. The thousands of demonstrators outside Trump Tower were making access to the building more difficult, and everything was delayed. Furthermore, all of the people he needed to meet had to enter secretly since the deals they were working on required ultimate discretion before the press swooped in and ruined things. He looked over the names—Juan Rodriguez from Cuba, the Bronsky brothers from Russia, and a group of New York real estate developers. He noticed that Rodriguez was listed twice and he considered whether he should fire his secretary in the morning for this mistake, sue her, or just renege on paying her. The thought of screwing his secretary, this one only figuratively, gave him a slight feeling of power and satisfaction. But before long, his Secret Service guard announced that the Bronskys were finally here. The guard, who had once read a biography of Leon Trotsky, stood close to Trump during the entire meeting.

The Bronskys were both blond haired and blue eyed and almost as tall as Trump himself, but younger and slimmer. Ivan stepped forward and greeted the Donald with a cheerful, "We bring regards, congratulations, and best wishes from President Putin himself. He is overjoyed at your victory."

Responded Trump, "Yes, I'm sure he is, and I want to thank him for all of his help with, uh, well, you know . . . just, all his help." They all laughed and nodded.

"You know, President Putin himself kept his hands off your election, of course, so as not to cause a scandal, but that guy Assange really went wild. Not only does he really hate Clinton, but we now know that he has tons more emails and tax documents from those Democrats that haven't even seen the light of day yet."

At the mention of tax documents, Trump felt sick, knowing what the implication was for him.

But Pyotr broke the tension when he brought out a large tin, which had been carefully screened by security, and presented it. "Here is some of the best black caviar we still make in Russia, straight from President Putin himself. He would have sent some Stolichnaya, but he knows you never drink, so he sent a big batch of really good ice cream. We gave it to your tasters a little while ago."

"Thank Vladimir for me when you see him. So, to the matter at hand. You know my firm, which my children will take over soon, is really in a position to build some of the best hotels and casinos in the world, and there's no place we'd rather build them then out there. You had some trouble in Sochi, but I can guarantee you won't have trouble with my places. We can talk about Moscow and St. Petersburg later, but I figured we should start with Sochi."

Ivan added, "President Putin also suggested you take a look at Vladivostok. The city isn't very much, but being so close to Japan and China there is a lot of potential, especially for a casino for those high-rolling, what do you call them, whales?"

"Well," said Trump, "I've had some bad experiences with Asian whales in my Atlantic City casinos, but I'll look into it anyway. Besides, when I scuttle the Trans-Pacific Partnership everything in the Pacific will be up for grabs. Thanks for the suggestion. By the way, do you two represent Putin, the government, private businesspeople, or what?"

Ivan lowered his voice a little and said, "In Russia sometimes those entities overlap. Let's just say we have the authority to deliver the messages, which will be followed up later."

"Speaking of messages," added Pyotr, "I was asked to bring up some completely unrelated matter, now that we are here. We know that the Baltic States are part of NATO and as such are primarily interested in their common defense, but they have been increasing their military training and spending and we can't help but be a little concerned."

The idea of the tiny Baltic States threatening Russia was absurd, but as part of NATO they had a strength beyond their size.

"As you know," Trump said, "I've complained a lot about NATO members not carrying their weight and depending too much on US money and military. Give my assurance that when I'm in office I will look into this as much as politically possible."

With that, they all shook hands and said good night. The first meeting was done.

But he didn't have long to ponder the implications of the conversation before his next guest was ushered in.

"This is Juan Rodriguez," said the guard, again standing next to Trump. Rodriguez was an emissary from the Cuban government but didn't look like it with no suit or tie, just common clothing. Was this a disguise to fool the crowds outside?

"Mr. Trump, my name is Juan Rodriguez. I was one of the contractors who worked on Mar-A-Lago for you years ago. I did some of the wood carving."

Trump realized that this wasn't the Cuban he expected but he must have gotten in simply because he had the same name as the other scheduled guest. What would a contractor want with the president-elect of the United States?

"Welcome, Mister Rodriguez. You've come from Florida. We carried Florida, you know," bragged Trump.

"Yes, congratulations. But I came for another reason. When I set up my contracting business, I put every penny I had into it, and borrowed even more. You really liked the woodwork I did, and even offered me more jobs at some of your other places."

"That's right," said Trump. "I remember you now. That was great work. Did you ever bid on my other jobs?"

"Well," said Rodriguez sadly, "I never got paid for the Mar-A-Lago work. Someone in your organization said the work was poor and refused to pay until a lot of revisions were done. But the revisions were greater than the original work. We're still in court with your people, and, well, we are in a bad spot. My son, Juan Junior, has bad asthma. Obamacare is covering his bills for now, but our legal fees are just eating us alive. I'm doing other work, but it seems hopeless. I know from your book *The Art of the Deal* that you are a good man, a good businessman, and would not let this happen if you knew about it. That's why I took one of those discount buses all the way from Florida to speak to you personally. Can you help us?"

The whole conversation was making Trump uncomfortable, especially the part about the sick kid. It wasn't his fault the kid was sick. Why did this guy think he was going to get special treatment?

"I'll have my legal team get on this right after Christmas. I promise we'll see that you get a fair deal. It was nice to meet you and give my regards to your family. By the way, is your copy of my book autographed? Here's one with my signature." With that he picked up a copy of *The Art of the Deal* off a large stack on his desk, signed it, and gave it to Rodriguez.

"Thank you, Mr. Trump, Mr. President. I told my wife that you would understand if I only got a chance to speak to you," although Rodriguez himself didn't understand that Trump had no more intention to help him than he had to help the coal miners in West Virginia whose votes he got.

Donald settled down a bit when the next bunch of visitors came in. They were all real estate developers in New York, many of them richer than Trump, but almost none of them had very much name recognition to the general public. They did their business as quietly as possible and were very good at it.

Trump started with, "Welcome, gentlemen, glad to see you. I think I know every one of you. I think I understand why you're here. If you want to get in on the Trump brand, now is the time to do it when this can be done quietly, without the media."

Melchior Ebrahim, the leader of the group and a prominent developer, answered, "That's not why we're here. We have plenty of projects of our own. This is Christmas, and we figured that this is the best time for you to make a grand gesture, as we all have promised to do, and donate to the poor. A billionaire president who hasn't forgotten the needy is the right thing to show morally and publicity wise."

Trump, shocked, answered with, "Help the poor? My foundation gives plenty to charity. My family has built public housing and middle-class housing for decades. Haven't I done enough?"

Balthazar Saud, a very rich member of the Saudi royal family who got even richer in New York real estate, shook his head and said, "What your family business did years ago was nice, but you have not done any of that for quite a while. As for the foundation, many of us have given more money to that foundation, and our own charities, than you have. A public act of charity, especially on Christmas, would make questions of you being a miser go away once and for all."

Trump became more agitated as he raised his voice and yelled, "Bull! All this talk about me not giving is bull, put out by a biased media. I give lots of money, my own money, and everyone knows it."

Gaspar Temani, a Yemenite by way of Israel, and a prominent builder in Williamsburg, answered, "If you don't want to give outright charity, why don't you join us in our announcement tomorrow about a project for low-income housing in New York. The mayor is behind it, the newspapers are behind it, even a few community boards are behind it. There are lots of poor homeless in the city, and just a start in this direction would help. We can work out the details later if you'll give us a public pledge. And, by the way, since when did you start using words like *bull*? That's the mildest profanity I ever heard you use."

Answering the last, easy question, Trump quietly said, "My daughter told me to tone it down and get used to civil speech so I don't slip up in some diplomatic meeting. *Bull* is the mildest I can go. As far as the homeless are concerned, aren't there shelters, and for the troublemakers aren't there prisons?"

The group was speechless.

"Well, aren't there shelters? Aren't there prisons?" Trump repeated insistently. "Besides, even with my tens of billions of dollars I can't solve all the problems of the country. That's what government is for."

At the mention of "tens of billions" some of the group laughed, some coughed, and some rolled their eyes. Melchior ended the meeting with, "Well, if you reconsider, you can always send us a tweet," he said sarcastically. "Here's my business card. I wrote my address, home phone number, and cell on the back. Meanwhile, thanks for nothing."

As they left, one of them muttered under his breath, "I'm glad I'm a Democrat." The others laughed softly, and even the Secret Service agent let out a little chuckle before he caught himself.

Finally, the bona fide Cuban representative Juan Rodriguez was ushered in. He was dressed in a plain business suit, as expected. It wasn't a Brioni or Armani, but it was presentable enough.

Somewhat graciously Trump started with, "Condolences on the passing of Fidel. Although we had a lot of disagreements over the years, I know he meant a lot to those of you who stayed on the island."

Ignoring the patronizing insult, Rodriguez answered, "Thank you, Mr. President," unknowingly giving Trump a slight thrill on hearing that particular salutation. "I am here to address the proposal your people sent to us. I'm very sorry, but our government just can't accept your casinos back in Havana and Santiago in exchange for complete diplomatic recognition. It goes back to the days when we were viewed as an American brothel. Our people, at least the ones who stayed on the island," pointedly throwing Trump's words back at him, "would never stand for it."

Using his favorite line, Trump answered, "That's too bad. They would be *huge*—the absolute best casinos in the Caribbean, believe me."

"But, I do have a counterproposal. What if you closed Guantanamo Bay and used that? I know you have plenty of dark sites around the world for prisoners you can't release, and with a Republican in the White House instead of a Democrat, Congress would be much more cooperative. You have the infrastructure already there, and it can become a self-contained resort, like Cabo or Cancun. The land would have to return to Cuban sovereignty so that we can monitor and regulate the casinos so as to not return to the bad old days. But, if it works out, we can discuss Havana or Santiago later. We also have a very nice beach near the Bay of Pigs, although you might find that in bad taste considering its history."

Trump thought for a moment and carefully answered. "Don't worry, nobody has ever accused a Trump property of being in bad taste," he said with a straight face, "but that's quite a lot of potential, although the government oversight is a little annoying. Let me think about it, and one of my children will get back to you along with our State Department."

Rodriguez added, "By the way, Prime Minister Raul Castro sent you a little gift. I know you don't smoke, but this is a box of the best Montecristo cigars in all of Cuba. Maybe you know someone who would like them."

Trump thought that maybe Rush Limbaugh would enjoy these and lighten up on him. This was a time for mending fences.

They shook hands politely, although when out of each other's sight they both wiped their hands clean.

Although it was only 11:30 p.m., Trump was unusually tired. Most nights he could easily continue working until early morning, but for some reason at this moment he was beat. A good night's rest and he would be ready to meet the rest of the Christmas celebrants tomorrow down in Washington. He told the Secret Service agents he was going to bed and slowly walked into the large bedroom, with its four-poster, canopied bed. But something wasn't right. Some of the papers on his desk, the canopy of his bed, and even the curtains covering his window were jostling slightly, although he couldn't feel a breeze anywhere. He walked over to the window but didn't feel anything there, either. He made a mental note to sue the workmen who installed it years ago, but that would have to wait until tomorrow. He put on pajamas, pulled the canopy, and fell into bed, sleeping soundly in seconds.

His sleep didn't last long. He quickly woke to hear a hideous moaning coming from somewhere inside his bedroom. Was the building still settling? Were there demonstrators making noises outside, or had one somehow gotten into his bedroom? He reached for the gun he kept under his pillow and slowly pulled aside the curtains surrounding his bed. He had never been so frightened in his life as he was when he turned on the bedside lamp. Standing before him, the very image of a ghostly spirit, was his father, Fred Trump. He was almost transparent, as most ghosts are, in uncharacteristically shabby clothing, looking horribly depressed, and wrapped in a heavy chain around his waist.

"This can't be!" Trump said out loud. "It must be that taco bowl I had them send up. I knew these Mexicans were rapists, but at least I thought they could cook without giving me food poisoning. Wait until my lawyers get them in court."

"What's the matter with you? You don't know the difference between your father's spirit and a taco-induced hallucination?" the ghost said.

It was his father! The same stern, judgmental, critical voice, with the same look on his face convinced Trump that this was no dream or hallucination.

"How could this be? What are you doing here?" he said, as he put down his gun and got out of bed.

Fred, a little gentler now, said, "The jump into the spirit world is a lot bigger than going from Brooklyn to Manhattan. There are things here you can't imagine, believe me. As to why I'm here, it's to save you from my fate."

"Your fate?" Trump questioned.

"See these chains around me? Without realizing it, I forged them myself. Every betrayal, every sin, every moral failure added another link. These ledgers attached to the chains, and the bundles of apartment applications with racial notations on them, they all add to the chain I have to carry. Whether it's for eternity or there will be some end to it, I don't know. I only know I have this burden now, and you will have it too when your time comes. Chains, ledgers, bundles of paper, and that's just the stuff you did before. What you are about to do as president will be an even bigger burden for you."

Trump thought for a second and almost seemed to plead. "I wasn't that bad. Besides, the ledgers are handled by short guys in yarmulkes."

Fred shook his head, sadly, and said, "See, that's just the type of talk that gets you more links on the chain, not to mention those cracks about the Mexicans."

"I know," said Trump, with an air of resignation, like a child getting caught with his hand in the cookie jar.

"And all those contractors you stiffed and took into court."

"I know."

"And your wives and girlfriends."

"I know."

"And the racial discrimination with your rentals."

"Wait a minute," pleaded Trump, "you taught me those tricks. I didn't think them up myself."

"I taught you a lot of things that I'm paying for now," Fred said, pointing to his chains. "How to discriminate against African Americans without getting caught. How to get back at your enemies, or even friends or blood relatives who irritate you. How to trust nobody—nobody! I taught you all that, and I'm paying for it now. When your time comes, you'll pay for it, too," he said, tugging against the chain around his waist.

Trump was truly surprised and said, "*African American*? Since when did you get so politically correct? Next, you'll be saying 'N-word' when you mean to say—"

"Yes, I know," interrupted Fred, "but the afterworld can be pretty judgmental. You have to watch yourself before a slip of the tongue adds another few links to the chain."

Trump thought for a second.

"You did good things, too. Built a lot of housing all over the place. Doesn't that count? And most of us kids turned out pretty well."

"No, it doesn't count," said Fred. "Doing some good, especially when it's for your own benefit, doesn't get you a pass on your mistakes, crimes, or sins. And, as for most of you turning out well . . . ," now his sad face became even sadder and his eyes sunk to the ground, "even there mistakes cost me. I gave Fred Junior all the opportunity in the world, a head start in the real estate business, and all the help I could. What did he do? He hated the business, became an airline pilot, married a woman I disapproved of, and drank himself to death at an early age. I was so mad at him I virtually disinherited his whole family. Maybe I could have put less pressure on him and a lighter hand would have made him enjoy the business more. Maybe I could have been stricter and whipped him into shape. I'll never know. When you're a parent you don't have a lot of chances to do things over. I did the best I could."

With that he let out a loud, chilling wail that must have been heard all the way down to the Fifth Avenue sidewalk. Trump rushed over to the door of his bedroom and peeked out. The Secret Service agents were there and wide awake. They couldn't hear any of this conversation with his father, including the wailing. Both he and his father were somehow beyond the reach of the mortal world.

Trump pouted. "Well, you did like him best, at least for a while."

"Don't give me any of that birth order nonsense. You're responsible for your own actions. Fred Junior is gone, and you're here. That's all that matters. Besides, I'm here haunting you and not with your sisters and brother Robert. You're the one whose soul is at risk, not theirs."

"Okay, I'll take responsibility for my actions. I took what you gave and became the most powerful man in the world. There are tens of millions of people who love me, almost a majority of Americans," he let slip out, acknowledging the popular vote results to his father even though he had questioned them in public.

Fred would have none of it.

"Yes, and tens of millions who hate you. And hundreds of millions who fear you and the damage you could do. You don't see demonstrators outside Robert's house, or Maryanne's, or Elizabeth's, only yours," pointing to the crowds down on Fifth Avenue.

Trump became a little cocky, and drew on some of his college philosophy education.

"Well, isn't it better to be feared than loved?" he said, smiling as though he had made a clinching argument.

Fred stepped toward him, and with a cold, stern look in his eye answered, "Yes, you remember your Machiavelli very well, but not well enough. Maybe I'll introduce you to Machiavelli if I have a chance later tonight. He's been wandering around in torment like me for about five hundred years. He said it was better to be feared than loved, but above all it's important never to be hated. People who fear you will not oppose you without careful consideration of the risks and benefits. But people who hate you will do everything to bring you down, even if it hurts themselves. Look at what happened to Hillary. For twenty-five years she was accused of everything from enabling her husband's philandering to murdering her friend and betraying the country while Secretary of State. What happened? People who would be helped by her policies and proposals voted against her because they hated her, often without even knowing exactly why they hated her. They said she was a bitch, a harpy, and every other vague misogynistic insult they could throw at her. Now, there are tens of millions who feel that way about you, and you've only started your political career. What's going to happen after a few years of making decisions that will inevitably make some people even more angry with you?"

Trump was still confident and still thought he had a good answer. "I can't make every decision. I'll have to delegate a lot of authority to my appointees, and if any of them screw up I always have plausible deniability. Isn't that what you call it when you can blame someone else for your mistakes? I'll blame other people like Reagan did, or say I didn't know about it like George W. did. It won't reflect on me."

Fred was getting exasperated. "Don't you know that the buck stops at the White House? You'll be able to weasel out of a few bad decisions, but not one after another. Besides, your appointees are turning out to be quite a bunch. Fanatics, ideologues, billionaires even greedier than you, spineless sycophants" (the best kind, thought Trump), "if not racists and white supremacists. And, many of your decisions will be irreversible, setting in motion events you can't control. You make a mess of the economy, or start a war, or whatever, you can't go back to a bankruptcy or divorce court and ask for another chance. This is the presidency you chose for yourself and not just another spectacular business deal."

The reference to bankruptcy and divorce stabbed at Trump for a second, but he was used to diverting attention from these failings.

"Like you said, dad, I'll just do the best I can. I'm not perfect, in spite of what I claim in public. I'm a quick learner, and the more experience I get the better I'll fight off my enemies."

Fred let out another loud wail. "You're already forgetting what I taught you! It's not just your enemies you have to worry about, it's also your friends, or people who claim to be your friends. You've negotiated in the business world, but those guys in Washington have also been doing their own negotiating for decades. They know how to quietly slip provisions into bills to help out their favorite special interests, or into treaties, and, let's face it, you're too lazy to read all the details of these mind-numbing pieces of legislation. You'll delegate it to those around you who are as untrustworthy as that skinny viper Ryan in the House or Turtle Face over in the Senate. They would both love to replace you on some pretext with that fanatic Pence. As for being a quick learner, that may be true when you want to be, but you can also be pretty lazy and irresponsible at times. You don't even go to your daily security briefings, and you'll be carrying around the nuclear football in less than a month."

Trump could see that the future was going to be more complicated than he thought, but was still confident that he could control things. "I don't trust these people because they love me. I trust them, at least a little, because they owe me and I can ruin them if I want to."

"Oh," said Fred, "and who do you think owes you so much that he'll be loyal and dependable?"

Trump thought for a second. "How about Bannon? He owes me. I took him, that crackpot Breitbart site, and all the conspiracy nuts from the alt-right into the center. If Hillary had won, they would still be laughable and ignored."

Another loud wail. "Bannon! Don't you realize that he and all those right-wing white supremacists, anti-Semites, neo-Nazis, and . . . what's the word . . . deplorables who voted for you think they're responsible for your victory? To begin with, they slimed Hillary as much as possible for years, not to mention Obama, and spread every paranoid conspiracy theory that they could, including that born-in-Kenya one. They think *you* owe *them*. And, if you don't give them what they expect, they'll turn on you in a second. In fact, even if you do give them what they want they may still turn on you if they want even more or if someone else comes along and offers them a better deal. There are lots of billionaires out there with pet projects and big bankrolls that could buy their loyalty just as easily as you did. Bannon!"

"Okay, if not Bannon, then maybe . . . ." But as Trump thought for a while, he realized that everyone around him wanted something, whether a really right-wing Supreme Court justice, a government appointment, a government job, a fat government contract or subsidy, another war, or just recognition and publicity. There was nobody he could bring up that his dad wouldn't find fault with, except maybe his kids.

"Dad, this has been a fascinating philosophical discussion, but to what end? Maybe if I'm exceptional enough to get a visit from my dad's spirit I'll also get a break in the afterlife. It's not like the world is packed with ghosts and spirits. After all, I am a president and that should count for something."

"You think so, son? Come and take a look."

Fred slowly moved over to the window, dragging the massive links with him.

As Trump glanced out the window he was horrified. Visible for the first time for Trump, but invisible to everyone else, were spirits filling the sky and sidewalk below. He recognized many of them. Some were real estate developers whose practices were a lot worse than his dad's. Some were politicians who had been sent to jail, exposed in scandals, or who had their crimes and sins hidden from the public. There they were trudging up and down Fifth Avenue pulling massive burdens behind them. He even recognized a few mobsters from Atlantic City that he had done business with. One was accused of dumping a victim in the trunk of a Cadillac, and there he was helplessly trying to pull that Caddy across the night sky. Some had their chains around their waists, like his father, some around their necks, and a few around their genitals, which made Trump wince uncomfortably.

But, all the way down on Fifth Avenue he saw one figure that frightened him more than all the others combined. There was an old man, maybe eighty or so, who was dragging a really heavy chain down Fifth Avenue. On his shoulder was a small cocker spaniel. His hands were both up in the air in the V for victory pose. Somehow he could make out the well-illuminated names on the massive books that were attached to the chain. Some read "Pentagon Papers," one read "Secret Plan," and another read "Enemies List." At the very end of the chain was a small model of an apartment house. Wait, it wasn't an apartment house, it was the Watergate complex in Washington. This must have been some low-level bureaucrat from years ago, Donald thought. But, when he turned to his father, Fred's icy stare went straight through him and he realized—it was Nixon down on the sidewalk. Presidents weren't immune from damnation.

All his defenses were gone. He turned to his father. "Why are you telling me this? All this mental torture is for what? Do you think this can show me what to do and save me? I can't go through another night like this."

"Your night is only starting, son. What I've shown you is only the introduction. We can save you if you listen."

"We?"

"Yes, we. What I've shown you sets the stage, but before the night ends you'll be visited by three spirits. Each will help you understand what happened in the past, what is happening now, and what will happen in the future. Now if you go back to your bed you'll fall into a deep sleep until the first spirit arrives. Good-bye, son. Good-bye."

His father's image slowly disappeared. What Trump had just experienced had put him through a gut-wrenching emotional experience, but the thought of three more spirits was even more frightening. As commanded, he went back to bed and immediately fell into another deep sleep.

Chapter Two

Almost as soon as he put his head on the pillow, the alarm rang. It was midnight. He hadn't set the alarm, but the spirit world was in control now and it went off anyway. Even the mortal world's Secret Service agents in the next room couldn't hear it. As he got up, leaving the gun behind this time, he parted the curtains around his bed and saw a strange figure. It was a little old man, maybe seventy, wearing a New York Military Academy jacket. Wait, he thought, he can't be that old. *I'm* seventy. He also noticed that this spirit had no chains on him. So, it was possible to be in the afterworld and not be damned, he thought.

Tentatively he asked, "Are you the first spirit I'm supposed to meet?"

"Yes, I'm the Spirit of Christmas Past. I'm here to remind you of experiences of many years ago that shaped you into what you are today."

"President?"

"No—sinner," the spirit said curtly. "Besides, you're not president yet."

Trump walked over to the spirit and asked, "So, you are going to lecture me on my past behavior? My dad did quite a bit already."

"I'm not here to lecture you, but to show you. I'm going to take you back to events in your past, and they will speak for themselves. I'm a spirit . . . we can do that sort of thing. Leave your body here and hold on to my arm."

Trump turned and saw himself still sleeping in bed. He glanced in the mirror and realized that he had become as transparent as the spirit. Although shaken a bit, he touched the spirit's arm and was immediately transported to another scene.

He was in a classroom decorated with Christmas ornaments. He looked out the window and recognized the parade ground of Fordham University. It was Christmas Eve, and he was sitting across the desk from Father Timothy Flotsky, his philosophy professor.

Trump whispered to the spirit, "Can they hear us?"

The spirit replied, "No, they can't hear us or see us, but we can hear and see them perfectly. I've brought you here to see one of the pivotal periods in your life, when your decisions set you on the course you're on today. I mean, the course you're on in the future. Oh, you know what I mean."

Trump was a little confused as to why his story started here. "But what about the experiences of my childhood? Don't they count? My dad alternated between being distant and being overly strict. He even went so far as to send me up to that military academy whose jacket you're wearing just to get rid of me."

"And because you slugged your music teacher," the spirit added.

"I never did that! It was the lying media that made that up. But whatever the reason, he sent me away. There were plenty of schools in Brooklyn he could have sent me to instead of all the way up to Cornwall. He wanted to get rid of me so he could give the family business to my brother Fred Junior."

"Stop whining," said the spirit, "and didn't your father tell you to stop with that birth order excuse? As far as having a distant father, you're not the only guy in the world with that problem. Plenty of people had the same family situation, and we're not haunting their dreams tonight—only yours."

"Are you sure you're not haunting them?" Trump asked.

"Believe me," responded the spirit.

For a second, Trump thought the spirit was mocking him with his own words, and when he saw the slight smile on its face he knew he was right. But, he ignored the slight and turned to face the two mortals before him who were in a serious discussion.

Father Flotsky was a Jesuit priest with one PhD in physics and one in theology. He taught the Philosophy of Science course. In spite of being a priest he had a sharp and probing mind and was talking to the young Trump.

"Son, you have a really good mind if you want to use it. I've never seen someone so good at twisting words and sophistry. Your ability to analyze, if not abuse, language is right up there with the linguistic philosophers. You should consider a career in philosophy when you graduate."

"Father, with all due respect, I want more than intellectual accomplishments. My family is in business, so I was thinking of that. But I would also like some public recognition. I tried sports, and I was really good in high school, believe me, but when I came here I hurt my foot in football practice and left the team. It might be enough to get me out of the draft someday, if this stuff in Vietnam ever heats up, but it won't get me any public recognition."

Being pretty good in language himself, Flotsky focused on the real meaning of young Trump's words. "By recognition you mean fame. You want to be famous, not just accomplished."

Although feeling a little guilty, young Trump stood his ground and said, "Yes, Father, I guess it is at least a little fame that I want. I want to excel in something that people recognize. If I go into business, maybe I can do it there. But, the family business is in Brooklyn, and real estate in Brooklyn isn't exactly a path to fame and fortune. I tried sports, but after I hurt my ankle I started playing squash. Squash! Have you ever heard of a well-known squash player?"

Trying to reach the young student, Flotsky pointed out that Bertrand Russell was a famous philosopher and a Nobel Prize winner.

"He's only famous to other philosophers. The most mediocre quarterback will be known to more people than Bertrand Russell. I really appreciate your advice, and I'll think it over, but I have a lot of decisions to make and I'll do the best I can."

"Well, come back if you'd like to talk again," Flotsky added.

Immediately, Trump and his spirit guide were transported to another classroom. He was still at Fordham but was talking to Professor Martin Olds, his English teacher. Olds was very much out of place in the Fordham campus. As the country exploded with the turmoil of the Sixties, Fordham stayed a little on the conservative side, at least when Trump was there. While other campuses reeked of pot, Fordham still held beer blasts at the nearby Killarney Rose. While other campuses were having demonstrations on civil rights, the war, and other Sixties issues, Fordham was still immersed in football and basketball. But, Olds was different. He was a pure hippie, with a fashionable Nehru jacket, some love beads, granny glasses, and unkempt hair. He even lived in Greenwich Village.

Professor Olds and the young Trump were alone in a classroom and in deep discussion.

"You know, Donald," started Olds, "you really have a vivid imagination. Not only do you have a way with words, making them mean whatever you want them to, but the way you can make up facts out of your own vivid imagination is right up there with some of the Beats. Have you ever tried LSD?"

"Never heard of it," replied Trump.

"Psilocybin mushrooms?"

"Nope. No alcohol, no smoking, no pot, no nothing," said Trump proudly.

Olds was impressed. The young student's ability to conjure up images and present them as facts even when there was no relation to the real world was tremendous, almost surreal, without the aid of any psychoactive drugs.

"Such appropriate use of a double negative for emphasis. See, you have a lot of potential as a writer," suggested Olds. "Why not consider it? I'm doing some novel writing myself. I've been working on *Mr. MacIntosh, I Presume* for the last fifteen years or so. It keeps growing and will probably be over a thousand pages. I guess it just got away from me."

Trump couldn't resist. "Maybe it was the LSD?"

Olds laughed at the joke and the sarcasm. "Maybe, maybe. I realize the trouble you have putting together a ten-page term paper, so if you don't like thousand-page novels, maybe poetry? Poems can be as long or short as you would like. And a successful poet is a hit with the chicks."

Trump liked the sound of that but then said, "Yeah, but an unsuccessful poet isn't. And these Thomas Moore Bronx Irish Catholic girls never put out."

"You don't know the right ones. And besides, you have to be a little aggressive and grab them by . . . well, never mind, I said too much already," Olds said, with a smirk.

But as Olds thought about it, he realized that maybe the straight-looking Trump really wasn't cut out for a world of poetry and counterculture. He was more Brooklyn than Bleecker Street. It really was a shame, considering the young man's imagination and ability to transcend the real world at a moment's notice.

"Well, Donald, I have a creative writing seminar in the fall. You'll be a junior then, right? If you change your mind, let me know and I'll make sure you get in. Peace."

"Yeah, Professor, peace," responded Trump.

Yet another classroom and another professor. Professor Gatsby was a business professor, tall with blond hair and blue eyes. He looked a lot like the young Trump, and because he taught business he caught the students' attention quickly.

"You seem to have a knack for business. Do you have any experience?" asked Gatsby.

Answered the young Trump, "Well, my grandfather was in lots of businesses, including real estate, and my dad has a big real estate business in Brooklyn. I've helped out in his office a few times. I enjoy it."

Gatsby digested this information and observed, "So you would be a third-generation real estate developer, or at least a businessman of some type. That's pretty good, you have a leg up, and there is still a lot of real estate in Brooklyn to be developed. I've done some work out on the North Shore of Long Island, but there's plenty in the city, too. You could make a decent living."

Trump laid his cards on the table and said, "Actually, I'd like to do more than make a decent living. My dad built up the business a lot, and I think I can take it even further. There's lots of government money for urban renewal and maybe even, if I'm lucky, some projects in Manhattan."

"Well, you're certainly ambitious enough. How do you like it at Fordham?"

Trump was cautious. "It's good enough, but I always liked the idea of being in an Ivy League school. I'd also like to get out of New York for a change, but not too far out. Do you have any suggestions?"

After a second Gatsby said, "The Wharton School is down in Philadelphia, not too far, but out of the city. With your grades it would be a long shot, but maybe your background might help. And, if you can't transfer as an undergraduate, maybe you can get a master's down there. When the children of successful businessmen want to go into the family company, it can usually work out pretty well."

"Not always, Professor, not always," Trump responded, thinking of Fred Junior.

This time, the spirit and Donald weren't whisked away. Trump turned to the spirit. "I was only there a few years, why is Fordham so important?"

The spirit looked somber, even for a ghost, and said, "It wasn't the location that was important. It was the decision you made. You could have stuck it out in sports. Maybe football if you healed up. Probably not squash for the reasons you gave, but maybe something else."

"Rugby? Soccer?" asked Trump.

"I don't know. Damn it, Donald, I'm a spirit, not an athletic coach. But that was only one option. Philosophy, writing, who knows what else you could have done?"

"But how can you make a living doing those other things?" asked Trump.

"What do you mean by making a living? If you mean getting filthy rich, probably not, although I think Noam Chomsky does pretty well with his books," suggested the spirit.

Commie, thought Trump.

"Besides, with your father's inheritance, which you are pretty sure of getting, you could do okay in any field. You don't see your sisters or Robert applying for food stamps, do you?"

"I think they're called SNAP now," corrected Trump.

"Well, quite a policy wonk you're becoming. Maybe there is some hope. Anyway, your ability and ambition were only starting in college. Your viciousness hadn't really started yet. You needed a master of that type of thinking to hone you to a fine edge. For that you needed Roy Cohn."

Now they were transported to a new scene.

A somewhat more mature Trump was sitting across a desk from Roy Cohn discussing legal matters. Trump was nervous, and Cohn was confident, even cocky. Trump started the discussion.

"You know about all these anti-discrimination suits the Feds are bringing against us landlords and developers. They send in a black family, and we turn them down, and then they send in a white family, and we accept them. The fact that we still send the black tenants to perfectly fine all-black apartment houses and the whites to equally fine all-white ones doesn't help much. Something about separate is not equal. They do this a few times, and they've shown a pattern of discrimination. The other developers are giving in and putting consent agreements into effect. You know, we will advertise in minority newspapers and rent anything to anyone with the money. I've been advised to do the same, since they have a ton of evidence against our family firm, but I just hate to give in. I'd rather fight. What kind of deal can you negotiate with the Feds for me?"

Cohn looked Trump straight in the eye and said, "Negotiate? Why negotiate anything? If you want to fight, you've come to the right guy. I love a good fight, too."

Trump was overjoyed. "So, you think we can win this?"

"No, they've got you dead to rights. You're screwed, and not in a good way. But, I'd advise you to fight so you don't get a reputation as a pushover. If the Feds, or any prosecutor, knows that you'll give in when you're guilty, then you might negotiate when you might be guilty. But if you fight, and fight vigorously, when you're absolutely guilty they'll hesitate to come after you again. You'll be much, too much, trouble. So maybe they'll pass you by later on the iffy cases and go after the low-hanging fruit, the other developers."

Trump began to understand. "So if you get a reputation as a fighter, no matter what or when, it will stick to you and scare off your opponents."

"You've got it," said Cohn.

Trump thought for a few seconds. "Well, I assume this will cost a little, but in the long run it might be worth it. Tell me, can this work under other circumstances? What if somebody says something about me in the press and I have a reputation as a suing machine? Will that scare people off? And if business partners, or even people I've contracted with for work, are in, let us say, a dispute over payment, a reputation like this could work there, too."

Cohn smiled broadly and said, "Now you've got it completely. And yes, it will cost you quite a bit for a fight like this, so I've got to ask you if you're in it to win it or will you chicken out?"

"I'm in it to win it, even if it costs me. I came here because I knew you were a fighter, I knew you were politically connected, and I knew you were connected in other ways that I needn't go into," said Trump. "But if I do this too often, everybody will know I'm a deadbeat and won't do business with me in the first place."

Cohn explained carefully, "Just because the government knows you're tough—okay, maybe a deadbeat in some ways—that doesn't mean the rest of the public has to know. We have these things called nondisclosure agreements where you don't have to admit to any type of wrongdoing publicly, even when you give in and admit it secretly. It's very convenient."

Again, Trump understood quickly. "So when you want to be tough, you can be tough without actually getting a bad reputation. Very nice."

Cohn put his arm around Trump and said, "Yes, very nice, indeed. But, remember, you can only pull this stuff with your enemies. With your friends you have to be a little more dependable. In our businesses it always helps to be connected in every way possible. Take politics, that's how I started. You have to pick your allies carefully, only the strongest and smartest are useful. Take the Brooklyn machine, for example. This guy Meade Esposito runs it with an iron fist and knows just what he's doing. He's strong and smart, the kind of man that will never go to jail and never take any of his allies with him. Those are the kind of guys you want. There's a few new, up-and-coming guys in the Bronx—Stanley Simon and Stanley Friedman. The same with them—strong, dependable, nobody will ever touch them. So, if you ever do anything up there, make sure you take care of them. And, in the construction business, well, you know what kind of guys are in that."

"I do, indeed," said Trump. "I do, indeed. Roy—may I call you Roy?—I think this is the start of a beautiful friendship."

Cohn followed with, "I don't know a lot about you, Donald, and yes, you can call me Roy. You have a family out in Brooklyn or here in the city?"

"No, I'm not married."

"Oh?" said Cohn with interest.

"Yeah, there are too many beautiful women here in the city. My favorites are blondes from Europe."

"Oh?" said Cohn with disinterest. "Well, I guess we have to enjoy ourselves as much as possible. After all, both our jobs are tough, and it takes tough men to be successful. We can't expect to project strength if we are a bunch of ballet dancers."

Trump laughed and asked, "You know a lot of ballet dancers?"

"Quite a few," answered Cohn.

"You like those skinny women?" asked Trump.

"Not really," answered Cohn, with a scowl.

With that, the spirit turned to modern-day Trump and explained, just in case it wasn't already clear. "Cohn was true to his word. He fought the Feds, accused them as publicly as possible of having a vendetta against you, of malicious prosecution, of having a very weak case, and everything he could think of. Of course, you lost and had to accept a consent decree, but you established yourself as a fighter who never backed down, whether you were right or wrong. You still have that reputation."

Trump was puzzled. "Is it a bad thing to have a reputation as a fighter? To stand up for my rights, or at least for my financial interests?"

The spirit was growing more frustrated. "I said you never backed down even when you were wrong. Do you understand the meaning of the word *wrong*? It means something that is immoral, a sin, harmful to other people. That's what this whole night is about. The things you do, and are about to do as president, aren't just an expression of your needs and wants, they also affect other people. They often hurt other people. You need more convincing."

Suddenly, they were on a beautiful beach. Although spirits, they could both feel the warm, Cuban breeze. On the beach was a young couple standing beside a large rowboat that contained a few oars, a mast with a sail attached, and numerous packages of food, water, clothing, and other supplies. Carmen Diaz and Juan Rodriguez had just gotten married, but economic conditions in Cuba were limited and they were ready to make a desperate attempt to sail to Florida. Running up the beach was their cousin, also named Juan Rodriguez.

The cousin called out. "Juan! Carmen! What are you doing? Are you crazy? You'll get killed!"

Trump turned to the spirit and asked, "Why are they speaking English in Cuba?"

Matter-of-factly, the spirit answered, "We have excellent translators in the afterworld. It wouldn't make much sense to send you a warning if you couldn't understand it."

Married Juan answered. "We're going to America. Don't try to talk us out of it. I can't make a living here in this economy. How am I ever going to get ahead?"

Cousin Juan answered with, "America is heartless if you don't have money. And it's dangerous."

Carmen joined in. "Cousin Miguel fishes in these waters all the time. He says the weather forecast is good, the currents are in our direction, and we should be in Florida in a few days. All we have to do is walk on US land and we will be given asylum. And you see this boat—Juan built it himself. You know he is the best carpenter in the village, so this boat is as dependable as those old Coast Guard boats. Besides, lots of Cubans have done well in Florida over the years, and there's no reason we can't. We both work hard, and there's enough construction there to keep us busy forever. The US system is strong and fair for someone who isn't afraid of working hard."

Cousin Juan wasn't convinced. "Lots of the Cubans who are doing well there were doing well here, too, even if they weren't getting rich. After the Revolution all the professionals, businessmen, and people with money left. But a lot of the Marielitos and others didn't do so well. Some ended up poor, some in crime, and some dead. Juan, you could go to college here for engineering, completely free. And Carmen, when you have your family medical care is free here, not to mention the milk mothers get when pregnant. The Yankees won't give you that."

Married Juan answered angrily, "You don't know what you're talking about. Medical care in the US is the best in the world. Even if you can't afford it, there are plenty of emergency rooms that give care to anybody who needs it, free of charge. And there are lots of colleges there, too. Our kids can go to school with scholarships and never have to pay anything or owe any money. What do you have here? Some low-paying job with the government? *Fugetaboutit!*"

"*Fugetaboutit?* You're talking like a Yankee already. Yes, I'll stay here. I've already got a job with the Ministry of Tourism. We're trying to get foreigners to come here for vacations."

"Vacations?" said Carmen. "What about the embargo? Americans can't come here, and they can't have hotels or casinos here, either."

"I'm not talking about those Mafia-run whorehouses the Americans had here," said the cousin. "There are lots of Russians, Europeans, and even Canadians who will come. You wait and see. And these will be controlled by us, not a bunch of mobsters."

With that, it became clear that none of them would change their minds. The Rodriguez newlyweds were risking everything to go to the US, and the cousin was just as determined to stay in Cuba and try to build it up. They all embraced tearfully before the couple got into the boat and pushed away. The stay-behind cousin and the two spirit onlookers stood on the beach until the rowboat was out of sight.

Trump turned to the spirit. "Those cousins . . . ."

The spirit nodded. "Yes, you've met them both. The one in the boat is the same guy you stiffed on his construction contract, and will still be stiffing for years to come, as you will see later tonight. The other one was the same emissary you met in your apartment. His determination not to let in the sleazy casinos of the bad old days didn't make him completely negative about your proposals. But, it's clear here and in the future that he won't just give you a blank check for what you want."

Although Trump feared what would be coming later in the night, he was getting impatient. "All this is ancient history, except maybe those Rodriguez guys. I've come a long way. The past is past, and the present is present. What now?"

The spirit nodded. "The past is past, and the present is present? Well, maybe you do have a way with words, or at least taking a complicated idea and distilling it into a soundbite. But, my time here is over. I've only been able to show you a few pieces of your past, but maybe later you'll see why they're significant. Good-bye, Mister . . . I mean, President Trump. Go back to sleep for a while."

With that, he slowly faded away and Trump's spirit rejoined his body in bed.

CHAPTER THREE

The alarm buzzed almost immediately. He looked at it and saw it was still midnight. The spirit world had made time stand still, and he realized he couldn't run out the clock on this evening's ordeal. It would last as long as necessary to teach him whatever lesson he was fated to learn.

He pulled aside the curtains again, but this time saw nothing in his room. He looked around and was sure he was alone. But, there was a bright light coming from under the door. Those contractors were told to make the door flush with the floor and so he made a mental note to look into suing them tomorrow. Well, tomorrow was Christmas, so maybe he would have to wait a day or two. In any case, he was curious about the light. His spirit rose up out of his body, as it had done before, and he walked to the door.

When he reached to open the door, his spirit hand went right through it. I must be getting pretty good at this spirit thing, he thought. But, he immediately realized that he was getting a little arrogant, even for him, and he knew that modesty was probably one of the values these spirits were trying to teach him. He slowly and carefully proceeded through the door, and was greeted by a wondrous sight.

Seated on a massive throne of gold, Trump's favorite color, was a larger-than-life, Santa Claus–type figure. He was dressed in a big red Santa suit, with white trimming, and sported a matching white beard. He was heavy, probably with a body mass index even larger than Trump's, and he let out a jolly, if somewhat creepy, loud laugh, which the wide-awake Secret Service agents didn't seem to notice at all, just like they didn't see this spirit or Trump.

Surrounding him on the floor were piles of gifts in every type of wrapping, along with large plates of food. There were large hams, broiled geese and turkeys, numerous cakes and Christmas candies, chestnuts and fruits, piles of yams and baked potatoes. Off in one corner was the tin of Russian caviar Trump had received earlier. Was this some type of message? He wondered. In another corner there was a plastic container of food with a glatt kosher symbol on it. How did that get here?, he wondered. Then he realized that Jesus was Jewish and maybe it was symbolically for him and his family, or something like that. Scattered around were a few trays of lasagna, Polish sausages, Chinese dumplings, and, of course, sushi. This was New York, and a multi-ethnic feast was certainly appropriate, and especially appropriate for the next president of the United States. Damn it, he thought, there goes that arrogance thing again.

He turned his attention to the immense spirit on the throne.

"I am the Spirit of Christmas Present," he bellowed. "Come a little closer and see all that I have brought with me. Pretty impressive, eh? It's almost as good as one of your brunch buffets at Mar-A-Lago," he said with a loud laugh.

Trump cautiously approached the spirit and said, "I guess you're going to show me what's happening right now. Too bad we don't have time to sit and eat. This food looks delicious. Oh, and I like the Russian caviar, and kosher meal for the Christ kid, and all this other symbolism. Very well done, I'm truly impressed."

"I'm glad you like it, Mr. Trump, but there's more symbolism here than just the food and this gold throne I'm sitting on. Did you stop and think why we've come to you on Christmas, of all days? There are plenty of nights between the election and the inauguration—why is this night different from all other nights?"

Trump thought for a second and answered, "Something about the Christ kid, something holy, something spiritual?"

"Very close, Mr. Trump. You see, it's not enough for us to show you the error of your ways. We also are here to show you the benefits of having an alternative set of values. We can't replace something with nothing, but we can replace greed with generosity, suspicion of everyone with love of your fellow man, vengeance with forgiveness. There's no better day of the year to do it than today. Take hold of my arm, and you'll see what I mean."

With that, the spirit got down from the throne and walked toward Trump. The spirit towered over Trump and was actually a little intimidating, though smiling and laughing all the time. There was also a warm glow that seemed to envelop the spirit. The warmth of Christmas? The spirit of Christmas? There wasn't time for Trump to think as he quickly held onto the spirit's arm as directed. They whisked off immediately.

They were in a middle-class-looking living room. It was neat and clean, with average furniture well below the standards of even the lowest rent Trump hotel room. But, it looked practical. On a bookstand was a picture of Jesus pointing to his bleeding heart. Three people were there. One was a boy of about eight or nine, dressed in a light but clean coat and puffing on an inhaler while mildly wheezing. Another was a young teenage girl, not yet fully into womanhood, but not fully a child either, also in a light coat. The third was a grown woman facing away from Trump. She was slim with a nice figure, but before he could give her a number rating she turned and walked to the kids.

He was surprised. It was Carmen Rodriguez. He was also surprised at how little she had changed. True, on the sunny beach, tanned, in a light dress she was an 8.5, maybe even a nine, here she was down to a 7, or maybe 7.5 tops. But, it was definitely her, and she was hurrying. Trump felt a little ashamed, very little, for thinking this way—old habits die hard.

"We'll be late for midnight mass. Hurry up, Maria, Junior!"

Just then, her cell phone rang and she rushed to answer it.

Carmen was all smiles and excitement when she picked it up. "Juan, where are you? Did you get to see him? Here, let me put you on speaker phone so the kids can hear," as would both spirits.

"Yes, I met with him. He was really nice, not like they talk about him in the papers. He said he would talk to his lawyers and we would get a fair deal. He even gave me an autographed copy of his book. Isn't that great? Anyway, this bus will take forever to get back to Florida, so I might not get there until the day after Christmas. I'm sorry, Carmen, kids, but this was important. Listen to your mother. Love you!"

The kids yelled back, "Love you and Merry Christmas!"

"We're going to midnight mass if we hurry. It probably just started. We'll say a prayer for you."

"And for our relatives in Cuba. I hear cousin Juan is doing well down there."

"Okay, we'll pray for them, too," said Carmen.

"And a prayer for President Obama, now that we have Obamacare for the kids," said Juan Senior.

"Of course we'll pray for the president. I know I've complained about it before, but at least the kids are covered, so I'll pray for him and his family."

"And say a prayer for Mr. Trump, too. I think he's going to come through for us."

Carmen's tone changed dramatically. "Say a prayer for Trump? Are you kidding? He's the reason we're in this mess. He's the reason you lost your business and spend half of your time in court and the other half getting those lousy jobs. He's the reason I'm waitressing forty hours a week. Pray for him?"

Juan was pleading over the phone. "But it's Christmas. If there's any perfect time to forgive people, it's now. If you say it during midnight mass, maybe it will count for more."

She was still mad, but slowly agreed. "Alright, for Christmas. I'll forgive him until he gives me a reason not to. I'll pray for Trump."

"And his family."

"Okay, and his family. Maybe they'll turn out different. Bye! We have to rush. I'll see you in a few days."

She hung up the phone and was starting to rush the children out the door when the spirit turned to Trump and said, "Take a close look at those children, and tell me what you see."

Trump still had a lump in his throat over Carmen's promise to pray for him and his children. But he wasn't ready for what he saw when he took a closer look at her children. They both had black hair and a dark complexion, even darker than his orange tan, but their features were familiar. Maria looked like Ivanka, his daughter, and Juan Junior looked like Donald Junior, his son.

He turned to the spirit of Christmas Present angrily and said, "This is a trick! One of your spirit-world tricks like making time stand still or making us invisible. Am I supposed to identify with them because our kids look alike? 'We are the World,' or 'It Takes a Village,' or whatever come-to-Jesus epiphany I'm supposed to have?"

He stopped short and caught himself. Of course that was why this was done. To exactly make the point on the common humanity of people. This was one of the lessons of Christmas, specifically Christmas, that he needed to learn. But there was so little they had in common, no matter what day of the year it was.

"Spirit," said Trump slowly and, surprisingly, reflectively. "We come from such different worlds."

The spirit was sympathetic. "Yes, you've come from different worlds. But it's easy to feel commonality with people who are carbon copies of you. It's harder to be sympathetic to people who are different, but not impossible. You can do it if you try. You have everything, and they are struggling. You can raise your children in security, but they have to worry about providing for their children every day. You understand this intellectually, even if you don't feel it in your gut just yet. But, you will."

For a second the old Trump returned. "Well, if they're struggling maybe she shouldn't have gotten pregnant. And by the way, using a carbon copy metaphor is a little stale, don't you think?"

The spirit chuckled. "See? Maybe you should have been an academic. Anyway, they were secure before they met you. Juan's business was going well—maybe not *huge,* but pretty well when they first had the kids. Then he did business with you, got stiffed, and now he's in well over his head."

As Trump was thinking this over, the spirit reached out to him and touched his arm.

Their next location couldn't have been more different. It was a spacious, well-lit conference room with lots of tables and chairs that had been pulled to the sides to produce a big, open area in the center. There were lots of men of all ages, and lots of beautiful women. Many were dancing in the middle of the room, and everyone seemed really happy.

Who were these people? They were all white, so for a second he thought he was in some alt-right white supremacist gathering, but there were no neo-Nazi decorations, just Christmas-style ornaments. He looked at the people in the center of the room and saw a few of the men doing that Russian dance in which the men squat down and kick out their legs in front of them. The Russian dance? He looked around the room again and saw empty bottles of Stolichnaya vodka all over the place. The buffet table was filled with big bowls of black caviar, like the type he had received earlier in the evening. There was fresh-baked Russian bread, which somehow he could smell, and fresh butter for spreading. On the side there were hot pierogi-type dumplings with more bowls of butter, sour cream, and more empty Stoli bottles.

They all were celebrating Christmas, he thought, but then remembered that in the Russian Orthodox Church Christmas is celebrated in January. What are they so happy about? Clearly, they were well lubricated from the Stoli. He realized why they were so happy when he looked up at the head table and saw the one person in the room who wasn't drinking: Vladimir Putin. They weren't celebrating Christmas but Trump's election. Putin was smiling and was talking to the Bronsky brothers in perfect, spirit-translated English. They were exhausted from flying overnight from New York to Moscow. Trump figured that this must be Christmas Day already, or maybe the day after. More spirit-world time tricks, he thought.

Ivan was speaking first. "Mr. President, I think it went well. He was as slippery as usual, and we didn't believe a word he said, but the ideas you suggested are well planted in his head. He wants to start his casinos in Sochi, test them there, and then branch out to St. Petersburg and Moscow. He even liked the idea of Vladivostok, especially when we pointed out the potential Asian clientele."

Putin nodded and smiled, saying, "I guess he's never been to Vladivostok. Well, that was good for a start, and how did you bring up the other end of the bargain?"

Pyotr spoke now. "We just got right into it. We were able to bring up the Baltic States, and I swear we did it with a straight face, just like you told us to. He took the bait and said NATO wasn't carrying its weight. He was noncommittal but seemed pretty open to the idea of backing away from them, at least a little. For some reason, he seemed to like the idea of screwing his friends."

"Well . . . ," said Putin, "when Lenin coined the phrase 'useful idiots' he couldn't have come up with a better description of the man who will soon be—soon be—" He started to choke up a little at the prospect of a Trump presidency, and actually let out a small tear, which quickly froze as it rolled down his cold, heartless, reptilian cheek. "The President of the United States. And the other matter?"

Ivan laughed as he said, "He opened it up himself, I think at the very beginning. He thanked you for all your help, without ever saying what the help was. He's stupid, but not so stupid as to openly acknowledge what we did, even when we all know what we did. And, you'll love this, when we implied that Assange might have hacked copies of his tax returns, in addition to all that Hillary stuff, he absolutely turned white."

Putin leaned back in his chair and in an almost philosophical manner said, "You know, people say I like violence and force. What they don't realize is that subtle blackmail can sometimes be more effective, and even more enjoyable, than force. It's like the sophistication of a stiletto instead of the crudeness of a club. He'll think twice before opening that can of worms. Speaking of cans, did you give him the two cans of caviar I sent?"

Pyotr looked a little hesitant but admitted, "Well, we gave him one can, and that big drum of ice cream you sent, but we traded the other tin with a guy from the Cuban Ministry of Trade. He gave us a good box of Montecristos. I know you don't smoke, but someone around here might like them. And, symbolically at least, it was nice to start double crossing Trump right away, without him even knowing it."

They all laughed. Trump angrily turned to the spirit. "So, they're laughing at me already. I'll show them—I mean, I'll reconsider my options at the first opportunity."

"Yes, that sounds a little better," said the spirit. "But you haven't heard it all yet."

They both turned back to the three Russians.

"Speaking of Assange, did you get him on the phone yet, Boris?" said Putin.

One of his minions approached and handed him a phone.

Putin was all smiles. "Julian, comrade, it's so good to talk to you. Yes, it couldn't have worked out better in our wildest dreams. And thanks for the tax returns. We haven't even started using them, but we already have him intimidated. Yes, of course, fifty million in Switzerland and fifty million in the Cayman Islands, just like we agreed on. By the way, if you can get out of your present situation and come over here we will give you another fifty million, and introduce you to Edward Snowden who would love to meet you. So would Anna Chapman, you know that tall, good-looking redhead that we had over in the US? No, don't worry, our laws on condoms aren't as strict as those uptight Swedes, you won't have to be that careful. Well, nice to speak to you and you have our gratitude. Maybe we'll work together again if he gets out of line. Bye, for now."

Pyotr was in awe. "What luck we had to get him working for us, and all it took was a hundred million."

"Not all luck, little grasshopper." Putin, the Judo black belt, was a *Kung Fu* fan. "The money helped, of course, but what choice did he have but to work for us? The Americans were talking about espionage and even executing him. They were out for blood, the fools. If they had realized how easily he could have hacked into our computers for them, they could have tried to make some deal with him—a secret deal of course, but still a deal. I would hate to have Wikileaks getting into my old files when I was in the KGB, or at least the ones I didn't find and destroy.

"And we had no choice, either. If Clinton had gotten in, it would have been hell for us. After twenty-five years of Republican persecution, she was as hardened as you could get. Did you see her at the Benghazi hearings? Eleven hours of testimony, and they couldn't shake her. *Eleven hours!* I don't think the KGB could have broken her back in the old days. I can't imagine sitting across a negotiating table from her. We had no choice."

They all nodded until Boris cautiously came over with a tray of vodka shots. "Mr. President, I know you don't usually drink, but this is such a special occasion. Compromising the leadership of our main adversary doesn't happen every day. Please, just this once, lead us in a toast."

Putin hesitated, then grinned and reached for a vodka, as did everyone else in the room. "A toast to President Donald Trump. May he fulfill all our expectations!"

They all shouted, "Nostrovia!"

Trump turned to the spirit. "Sarcastic bastards. I guess your translators left it in Russian just to rub it in."

"Yes, they did, Mr. Trump. Yes, they did."

With that, Trump touched his arm and they were off again.

This time he recognized the scene immediately. He was in the White House, in one of the parlors. It was decorated with the usual Christmas lights and tinsel, and the tree in the corner was covered with ornaments, many of them gifts from foreign countries. Packages of various types were under it, still unopened. There was plenty of food on the buffet tables, but Michelle Obama's touch was evident. The eggnog and punch came both with and without alcohol, and all of them low fat. The meats and cheeses, roasted veggies (from the White House vegetable garden), and yams were at one end of the table with the cakes and candies at the other. It was almost as bountiful as the feast around the throne of the Spirit of Christmas Present, back in Trump's apartment.

Although there were security people and various servants and staffers all over, the media people had left for the night and the families were mostly mixing with each other. The Obama family was small, but the Trump family was massive with over a dozen relatives just within the immediate family. Everyone was relaxed and having a good time, even without the flowing Stolichnaya of the previous location. There was one thing missing—Trump himself, at least the recognizable, mortal Trump. Everyone was waiting, knowing that he was supposed to come down from New York City. When he called to say he was just too tired to travel, they were all disappointed, even the Obamas who thought a conciliatory gesture on Christmas Eve was just what the country needed. But, the grandchildren were falling asleep, as were some of the younger Trump children.

Trump himself was so happy to see everyone he almost stepped into the scene expecting to be recognized and acknowledged, but he stopped when the Spirit of Christmas Present held him back and spoke into his ear.

"Beautiful sight, isn't it? Too bad you had those business deals to clean up, I mean iron out. I think they will be having a final round of toasts before they call it a night. Maybe we can listen in," he said, almost mischievously.

They both walked over to the Obamas who had stepped to the side. Although President Obama and Michelle were smiling, they were also arguing under their breaths, beneath the happy facades.

Michelle was angry. "You want to toast to his success? Anybody with racism and sexism in his heart doesn't deserve a toast or best wishes, even on Christmas."

The president was softer. "I don't know how much of a racist or a sexist he is in his heart, all I know is that he's an opportunist, and an excellent one at that. He can change positions at the drop of a hat and convince people he's sincere. We knew he was a con artist, but we underestimated how effective he was. So what's the point of arguing it now? Should we lecture his family in his absence and look like sore losers? Should we preach at him like they did to Pence when he was up in New York a week ago? It would only allow him to play the victim again. We should be as civil as possible and let him have the time he needs to self-destruct."

Micelle wasn't convinced. "His self-destruction will take the country with him. Think of all the people he'll hurt. Think of the country. Now we pat him on the back with a toast like 'Let bygones be bygones'?"

"I know what he'll do," said the president. "Some of his appointees would like to go back a hundred years to before the New Deal, or maybe further to the Gilded Age. He's doing okay right now, but they usually do in the beginning. It took Reagan six years before he crashed the stock market and quadrupled the national debt. It took George W. eight years to destroy the economy, although he wasted no time starting wars. Trump's people will do the same, eventually. We have to work to pick up the pieces."

"You're pretty confident this cycle from conservative to liberal will keep going, aren't you?" she said.

"It's not conservative to liberal, it's Republican to Democrat. Reagan hurt the country, but Clinton cleaned it up. George W. hurt it even more, catastrophically actually, but we were able to clean it up. We have to hold together and not act like nasty jerks like them. It's Christmas, just tonight."

Finally relenting, Michelle nodded. "All right, in the spirit of Christmas I'll forgive and forget for twenty-four hours. Maybe even until the inauguration, but after that, no promises."

"All right, Michelle, just tonight, just Christmas," he urged.

"So, the spirit of Christmas succeeds again," said Trump, reluctantly.

"Yes, it did, but there's more," said the spirit.

They walked over to the other end of the room where the Trump family congregated. Melania was standing with the younger children, Barron and Tiffany, along with some of the sleepy grandchildren. The three senior children were talking as Trump himself glided over.

Donald Junior shook his head. "You know, I feel most sorry for him. Look at this get-together. A few months ago we were at each other's throats, us and the Dems, and now we're all together. But, he's up in New York, on this night of all nights. He couldn't leave those deals until next week?"

Ivanka agreed. "Well, he is just obsessed about leaving us with as few problems as possible. He has to fix up the Russian and Cuban deals before he hands them over to us so that we can spend our time on damage control and not have too much blame on our shoulders. Besides, he loves this type of deal making and maneuvering. This might be the last time he can do this without destroying the economy or starting a war. This stuff is harmless, relatively speaking. Let him have his fun."

Eric chuckled. "Harmless? Wait until people hear about the casinos in Budapest he's building with George Soros. The people will have a fit."

They all laughed, but Ivanka got serious. "No, *he's* not building them, *we're* building them. Remember, each one of us has to take the heat for one of them, either Cuba, Russia, or Budapest. We can divide them up later. But we may have a bigger problem with some of the evangelicals who think we should do more building for the poor, and not just casinos and condos for the rich. They're our allies, so we can't ignore them so easily."

Donald Junior just smiled. "Once dad's people get in, nobody will be building anything for the poor without big government subsidies, like grandpa got and started the business. And we'll be a lot more politically connected than he ever was. We might even make a killing with low-income housing if the tax breaks are big enough. Who knows, maybe we won't even have to pay taxes!"

With that, all three laughed.

Trump took this all in and said, with a tear running down his cheek, "I'm so proud of those kids." He then realized the spirit was giving him a cold stare.

"That's not why we're here," it said.

Their attention turned back to the children.

Ivanka spoke. "They've been so gracious, we have to give them some type of toast or thank you. It's only polite. Besides, it's Christmas. If there's any time of the year we can be generous and forgiving this is it, and it might not come again when dad's in office and making enemies. I'll do the honors."

With that, the two families approached each other. It was almost midnight, and some of the children weren't used to this late hour. Obama went first.

He raised a small glass of organic, low-fat, non-alcoholic punch and said, "Here's a toast to Christmas and to President-elect Donald Trump.

May he serve the country well." Although he'll never serve it as well as I did, Obama thought.

Ivanka raised a glass of spring water and responded, "Here's a toast to President Obama for his years of service and tonight's wonderful get-to-gether in the spirit of Christmas. We hope we can be as gracious as he has been," while thinking that she and her brothers were going to loot this city more thoroughly than the Visigoths sacked Rome.

"After all that fighting, they actually got along," said Trump with an honestly surprised expression. Against his basic instinct, the Christmas spirit was taking hold of him.

The spirit touched his arm, and they were gone. Now they were in some dark place, and it took a minute for Trump's eyes to acclimate. They were in some type of mine, next to a group of miners eating their meal during a break. They were covered with dust, except for their hands, which they had just washed somehow. As they ate and spoke to each other, Trump turned to the spirit.

"This looks like Appalachia during the Depression. Those miners look miserable and exhausted. And the smells down here! I hope none of this is methane."

The spirit shook its head no.

"Maybe it's further back. England during the 1800s, maybe. They look depressed enough, although I can't hear if they have English accents."

The spirit shook its head no again.

"Where are we?"

"We're in West Virginia, earlier this afternoon," said the spirit.

These couldn't be coal miners, Trump thought. He had seen lots of miners at his rallies. They were enthusiastic, energetic, and yelling his name at the top of their lungs. These guys looked beat, sore, and achy with hardly enough energy to lift a drill, let alone attend a rally. But, they had enough energy to argue.

Mike, the foreman, was talking. "I don't trust him, either, but at least he said he'd try to do something, bring some jobs back, or at least keep the ones we have."

Sam, the cynic, was in his forties, overweight and coughing occasionally, a symptom of the respiratory disease slowly developing in his lungs. "He can promise anything, but can he deliver? I don't believe it. The union, or what little is left of it, couldn't deliver, and they actually know the coal business. This guy's from *New York City* like the guy in that salsa commercial. He knows as much about coal as I know about building condos in Florida."

Adam, the youngest of the group, was much healthier looking, with blond hair like Trump's except a little shorter. "Well, if we don't trust him and he can't deliver, why did the country vote for him?"

Zeke, the oldest of the group, answered. "The country didn't vote for him. Hillary got a few million more votes than he did. The electoral college will vote him in. You guys talk like we're in a democracy where the will of the people rules and government can help you. Where have you all been since President Reagan?"

Mike spoke up again. "Well, maybe he can't deliver and maybe none of us trust him, but he's the only hope we got. Hillary told us the truth about coal? Well, I don't want to know the truth. Maybe like that line from that Tom Cruise movie, I can't handle the truth. But at least with Trump there's hope. We'll find out soon enough."

Sam couldn't resist adding a sarcastic comment. "Maybe if they get rid of the safety measures and government inspections that will make the mines cheap enough to keep open. We do still have safety measures and government inspections, don't we?" he said, looking around with a comic expression on his face.

The men laughed and slowly went back to work.

Trump turned to the spirit. "They don't trust me. They think I'm lying. They think I can't deliver, and they just voted for me because they didn't like Hillary. Did any of these guys vote for me?"

"They all did. Every. One. You're their only hope, even when that hope is a mere flicker. Whether or not you can deliver on your promises only time can tell. But that's not why I brought you here. Let's go upstairs."

They flew up through the earth and a little ways away from the mine to a large community hall with lots of Christmas decorations and a big, festive tree in the corner. Most of the people, but not all, were white, and most of the miners, but not all, were men. On one side of the hall was a buffet with lots of food, most of it homemade. On the other side was a big bar with almost every kind of liquor you could think of (again, no Stolichnaya), along with lots of soft drinks, coffee, and tea for the non-drinkers. All around the hall there were people talking, a few dancing at the far end near a small fiddle band, and lots of kids.

The kids were running up to a miner dressed as Santa. He was on a wooden, not gold, throne, and was giving out small toys and candies to the kids. Every once in a while he would let out a big, Santa-type "Ho-ho-ho!" The kids were having a great time, and Santa was enjoying it, too. Then Trump looked closer. It was Sam, Sam the cynic. The miner who didn't seem to believe anything was having the time of his life. Trump even noticed a bottle of iced tea next to him, that he sipped on now and then. He was sober as a judge.

"So, this Christmas spirit gives people hope for the future?" Trump asked.

"Absolutely not. These folks aren't idiots. They know life will be just as hard for them in a few days, or a few years, as they expect, even with a President Trump. They're doing this because at Christmastime you do things that give you simple pleasures, including helping others. You don't just get enjoyment from making a fortune, fame, power, the ability to hurt your enemies, or any of the activities you love. Helping others, and not just through a bogus foundation, is enjoyable. Studies have even shown that sometimes people get more enjoyment from giving than receiving. Oh, why am I telling you this? Just look at them. These people struggle every day and face a bleak future, yet they are having a better time than the folks in that White House party who have everything in the world."

Trump thought for a second. "So you're saying that the poor are really happy and the rich are really miserable in spite of being rich?"

"No, of course not. That's just a myth that we have in America so that the average person won't hate the rich and take political action against them. Rich folks live like kings in the US. This just means that at some times, Christmas for some, Easter for others, Thanksgiving for some, and maybe even Halloween, people get enjoyment and add meaning into their lives. You could, too, Mr. Trump. You could get enjoyment and find meaning by doing good and not just by doing things that will get you a few tons of chains around your waist, or around your whatever."

"But," continued the spirit, "these people voted for you. Let's go see a different group."

They instantly materialized in a very different location. They were in a small meeting room that was gaily decorated for the season. A small, plastic Christmas tree was in the corner, but no gifts. It looked like some type of medical facility as there were a lot of nurses in hospital scrubs, and nurse's aides in blue uniforms. They were all women. As they spoke to each other, Trump heard Spanish accents, West Indian accents, and a few Asian accents he couldn't place.

Most of the food looked homemade. He recognized the Latin pernil, rice and beans, and plantains, the West Indian fish stews and soups, and even the Korean kimchi because he once wanted to open a casino in Seoul, but there were a few noodle dishes he couldn't place. Maybe Filipino? He looked over at the liquor table and realized it lacked any liquor. Plenty of tea, soda, orange juice, and some weak-looking punch, but nothing alcoholic. There was also a big Christmas cake they were cutting up and passing among themselves.

Lydia, one of the Puerto Rican nurses, was cutting cake and talking. "I just want to have a good time, a good Christmas, and forget about the election until next year. Besides, except for the docs and the administrators, everybody here in the nursing home and the assisted living next door is union, not just the nurses and aides, but the maintenance, supply room, everybody. They can't hurt us, can they?"

Mutya, the senior nurse and the union rep, was more cautious. "No, they can't do anything to us unless they want half the nursing homes and hospitals in the city to walk out. But they have a lot of changes in mind for Medicaid and Medicare. The whole subacute rehab unit is covered by Medicare and the long-term unit by Medicaid. They start messing with them and who knows what will happen. When reimbursements got too low, some of those nursing homes in the city got closed and converted to luxury condos."

"But this is Brooklyn," said Mary in a thick Jamaican accent. "Who would want to build anything out here?"

Trump was a little annoyed at this insult to his homeland, but the spirit chuckled and motioned for him to pay attention to the conversation.

Mutya continued, "I was in the assisted living wing years ago when they got their drugs from Medicaid. Everything was easy except once or twice a month you would have to call in for a prior authorization for some med or another. Then the Feds took it over and privatized it to a dozen companies. Each one had different rules, regulations, phone numbers, paperwork, and formularies. It was a horror. We were spending at least an hour a day getting PAs, and sometimes we still didn't get what we needed. And that was just drugs. Can you imagine if every person coming in here had a different insurance company instead of straight Medicare? We'd be spending all day on the phone arguing over something or other."

Lydia jokingly yelled out, "Enough! Is this a Christmas party or a union rally? Come on, eat up, the evening shift will be here soon. And the maintenance department is starting their party right after that. They have the best parties in the whole place, and enough rum in the coquito to put us all in a coma."

"But wait," said Mary, "this is Christmas, so before we break up we should all have a toast to someone."

"Good idea," said Lydia. "Everyone take one person to toast, and we'll all join in. I'll toast Mutya. Even though she gets a little serious, like right now, she's the best rep we have when it comes to grievance procedures, and we do appreciate it."

Everyone raised their glasses and toasted Mutya.

"I've got a good one. Let's toast the Watanabe family. Every time they come in to see their mom, they bring cookies, and today they brought in a really big box for Christmas."

Everyone raised their diet sodas, coffees, teas, and bottled water to toast the Watanabe family.

Kim, the only Korean nurse, was smiling when she actually said, "Let's toast President Trump. He'll need all the help he can get, and we might as well get used to it. Besides, you never know what he'll do. He even tried to build a casino in Korea."

Everyone let out a roar. The Puerto Rican women started cursing in Spanish, Mary almost fainted, and Mutya just put her hand over her face. Fatima, over in a corner, her head covered in a scarf spoke up in a trembling voice. "That man is vile. Even though I have a green card and two of my kids were born here, I don't trust him. He would send me back to Morocco as soon as he'd look at me, and the people he appointed are even worse. And the only reason he didn't build that casino in Korea is probably because he couldn't find the right politicians to bribe."

Mary shouted down everyone. "Yes, he is a real piece of work . . . "

"Or of something else!" Lydia said to everyone's laughter.

"But he's our president," Mary continued, "and this is Christmas. This is the time to forgive and embrace all men."

"Men of good will, which certainly leaves him out," said Lydia.

Mary thought for a second and then said, "Well, let's go a little beyond the minimum. If we can open our hearts to someone who has no heart, then we're the better for it."

Everyone grumbled, but appreciated Mary's point. They weren't going to be on an equal footing to Trump, they were going to be better than him, by forgiving and blessing someone who may not have really deserved to be forgiven and blessed. They slowly raised their glasses, cans, and bottles as Kim repeated, "A Christmas toast and blessing to our new president, may his administration be happy and prosperous."

"And short," mumbled Lydia, thinking about 2020.

Trump turned to the spirit. "Well, this was a lot different from West Virginia, that's for sure. How many votes did I get here?"

"None, not one voted for you. But for a very brief moment, however halfhearted, they all blessed you. Even the Muslim women did. It's a strange thing to see how hopeful people can get on Christmas. Well, it's getting late, and I have to get you back to Trump Tower. You have another visitor coming. On the way there, we just have a few brief stops."

They flew out of the nursing home, instead of just materializing. Trump recognized the area. They were flying past the old site of Steepelchase Park where his father had one of his most well-known demolition projects. People were invited to throw bricks through the windows under the smiling gaze of Fred Trump and several attractive models. He was never able to fully develop the area. They were coasting just a block away from the minor league baseball stadium that actually did get built, when the spirit stopped them both short. They were standing next to an old building, under a scaffold, and near a small encampment of homeless people. Over the cardboard shacks and the people dressed in multiple layers of clothing in order to survive the December weather was a spray-painted sign that simply read "Trump Tower South."

He couldn't believe what he saw. Even here, they were celebrating Christmas. There was a small, decrepit-looking tree decorated with lots of tinsel. One of the people had a box of donuts and was handing them out. Another had a half dozen containers of steaming hot coffee, also being distributed. This was the simplest breaking of bread, or at least of cake, Trump had ever seen.

One of the men raised his coffee, pointed to the sign above, and offered a toast. "To our new president, may he not let us die too soon." They all laughed.

"They all think that I don't care if they live or die," said Trump, truly shocked.

"Well, if I didn't bring you here would you have thought of them at all tonight, here freezing on the street?" said the spirit.

"But they don't have to freeze," said Trump.

The spirit lost his jolly laugh and smile and said, "Yes, I know. Aren't there shelters . . . aren't there prisons?"

Trump's words thrown back at him weren't exactly unexpected. "At least they would get shelter and not freeze."

The spirit persisted on his cynical theme. "Yes, shelters and prisons would provide housing for a few nights. You know what else provides housing? Housing. Housing actually provides housing, and you build houses, or at least you did. Let's see, there was one more thing. What was that . . . what was that? Oh, yes, of course. You're president of the United States. The president of the United States might be able to provide a little housing."

Trump wondered if all spirits were this sarcastic. With sarcasm, your own words can be turned against you, and Trump has spouted out a lot of words in the last year and a half. But, before he had time to think up a counterargument, the spirit grabbed his arm and they were flying to Manhattan. Just before they reached Trump Tower, the spirit guided them all the way down to street level.

They were right in front of the Rockefeller Plaza ice rink, with the golden statue of Prometheus keeping an eye on the graceful skaters, and the massive Christmas tree towering over everyone. Although it was late, there were still plenty of people walking around the plaza.

Resorting to the Socratic method instead of sarcasm, the spirit asked Trump, "What do you notice about these crowds?"

Trump looked around. There were men, women, and children of all races, all ages, and apparently even from all religions judging from a small group of nuns, the occasional yarmulke, both Sikh- and Hindi-style turbans or Muslim head scarfs. What do they all have in common? he wondered.

Trump finally hit on it. "They're all having a great time. Look at them. There's no reason everyone of these people should be enjoying a Christian holiday. They've been fighting and killing each other for millennia, but here they are sharing something or other that's making them happy. Maybe it's spiritual, maybe cultural, maybe even materialistic, but they all seem to be one happy family. How did that happen?"

"How, indeed," said the Spirit of Christmas Present, as they material-ized in Trump's bedroom.

"There is one more warning I have for you, Mr. Trump." He moved close to Trump who noticed that the spirit's robe was billowing out and something seemed to be moving underneath. The spirit slowly opened his robe to reveal two small, thin children, dressed in rags and looking both frightened and threatening at the same time. How do spirits manage to do that? Trump wondered.

"This boy is Ignorance, and this girl is Want. Beware of both, but espe-cially the boy," said the spirit ominously.

Trump nodded his head and said, "Yes, I understand. The ignorance and want of the world can overwhelm even a president."

"No, no, no," shouted the spirit, "these children don't represent the world's ignorance and want, although there's plenty of that around. They represent *your* ignorance and *your* want. It's your own weaknesses that are represented here. Take a closer look."

Trump bent over to see the children and realized, although they looked like street urchins, they both had his face. They were manifestations of his personality produced by the magic of the afterlife.

"Making them look like me is a pretty unsubtle trick. By now I expected something a little more refined," said the clearly annoyed Trump.

The spirit shrugged his shoulders and said, "We're pretty good at visual tricks in the afterlife, so what's the sense of having them if you're not going to use them?"

"You're pretty good at throwing my own words back at me, too. I recognize that line from one of my interviews. But how can ignorance and want apply to me? I know what I'm doing considering I'll be president, and I don't want for anything."

The spirit slowly and sincerely explained. "Just because you know some things well, doesn't mean you can't be ignorant of other things, even important things. You didn't know what the nuclear triad was. High school kids who read the paper know that. Computer gamers know that. If I had more time I could go through all the important things that you didn't seem to know, and didn't seem to care about learning."

"At least I knew where Aleppo was," said Trump, making a small but snarky point. "But what about want—what could I want?"

"That's a good question, Mr. Trump. What do you want? Early in life you had plenty of money, but you wanted more than that. Then you got fame in the media and your name was a household word. But, you wanted more than that. Now you have power. You're the most powerful person in the world, at least symbolically. You've always wanted something more, and sometimes did some pretty nasty things to get what you wanted. Well, let me suggest that there is one more thing you should want, while you still have a chance to get it."

"What's that?" asked Trump nervously.

"Redemption," said the spirit.

CHAPTER FOUR

After the Spirit of Christmas Present delivered his verbal knockout punch, Trump fell back into his bed and into his body. His rest didn't last long, however. He heard a faint rustling somewhere at the other end of his huge bedroom. He parted the curtain around his bed again, climbed out, and slowly walked toward the sound. He soon was able to see the figure. It was entirely dressed in black, tall, thin, and standing completely still as Trump approached it. When he was a few feet away, he flipped on the wall switch and absolutely couldn't believe what he saw.

A black robe covered the spirit except for the face and hair. The spirit was a woman. Not only that, but she had the most beautiful face he had ever seen, by far, and he had seen a lot of beautiful faces in his time. She was, of course, blond, with piercing blue eyes, perfectly symmetrical in every way, gorgeous lips and sparkling teeth. She even smiled and produced two of the most beautiful dimples he had ever seen. He usually was a high cheekbone man, but this face was awesome, totally awesome. Furthermore, no matter how closely he looked, he couldn't see any makeup on her at all. The black robe was draped around her very loosely so he couldn't get an absolutely accurate idea about her figure, but, again, his experienced eyes quickly determined that she was both extremely voluptuous and yet perfectly proportioned, kind of like the Golden Ratio that mathematicians and philosophers talked about (his Fordham philosophy classes finally did have some value). He never thought he could honestly say this, but this woman was an eleven.

He slowly moved toward her to get a better look, when she spoke out, "That's close enough. You're not on the bus or in a locker room now, Mr. Trump."

He was shocked and almost fell as he quickly stepped back a few feet. Her voice was a perfect, accentless, Midwestern American one, like the broadcasters use so they sound universal.

Trump said, "For some reason, I thought you were going to be one of these silent types, you know, sending your message in ominous gestures. Even this black robe, although highly fashionable, even on Fifth Avenue, gives an air of mystery."

"Oh, the Orthodox Spirits of Christmas Yet to Come do that. I'm a Reform spirit. We love to talk. Besides, your future is very complicated and a few gestures won't do the trick. As far as the robe goes, I'm here to condemn your sins and save your soul—what was I supposed to wear? Pastels? Here, take my hand, we have a lot of travelling to do."

As she stretched out her hand, Trump noticed that she was wearing a wedding ring.

"You can get married in the afterlife?" he asked.

She laughed and said, "No, we don't get married. This is my decoy ring to ward off guys hitting on me. I usually don't explain this, but since wedding rings never made much difference to you, I might as well. Even when I'm on a mission to save someone's soul they can't help making a pass. They see a pretty face and start wondering what's under the robes, and I can't get them to focus on the matter at hand, even when it's eternal damnation."

Uncomfortably Trump remarked, "Yeah, hard to believe guys would think like that."

She continued, "Yes, straight guys, lesbians, sometimes even gay guys and straight women. It's amazing who'll come on to you. In your future lives when you're back as a woman, you'll understand better."

"Future lives?"

She was embarrassed but quickly answered, "Oops, I've said too much. Here, take my hand. Let's get going."

They flew out of Trump Tower and headed downtown, passing through the trading floor of the New York Stock Exchange and into one of the conference rooms. There were a bunch of executives from banks and trading firms. A few he recognized as members of his administration, and some he just knew by reputation. The men, and they were all men, were sitting around the table in earnest discussion.

The Goldman Sachs CEO spoke first. "Well, things were great when the tax breaks and speculation got us to 20,000, and I know we all cashed in then, but now with the crash we've all got to hustle."

Bank of America's CEO shook his head. "We all knew this was coming. I just wish I got the timing right. If I shorted the market, I could have made a fortune. Well, a bigger fortune, that is."

Wells Fargo's CEO was more practical and even a little optimistic. "My analysts tell me that it will turn around really soon, now that we're under 10,000. If not, President Pence, Ryan, and McConnell all told us we could get whatever support we needed. What's a few trillion here or there when you're too big to fail?"

Trump turned to the spirit. "President Pence? What happened to me? Is this really eight years in the future?"

"You'll see later on. For now, just listen," said the spirit.

"Gee, I hope it doesn't drive up the deficit too much, or get us in trouble with the law," said the Citigroup CEO, with a straight face.

They looked at each other for a second, then all let out a hearty laugh.

The JP Morgan CEO just smiled broadly and said, "If Obama didn't send any of us to jail, Pence sure won't. And the deficit really will be a big problem . . . once a Democrat gets in the White House. With Pence there, maybe not so much."

It irritated Trump to hear Pence's name again without knowing what was going on. What was his role in all of this, either during his presidency or afterward?

"Besides," Goldman Sachs said, "if the Feds don't come through, we have other friends who could help." He turned to three Asian men sitting in the corner, representing the three largest banks in China—really big banks.

"*Fugetaboutit,*" said one of the men. It was strange to hear a Chinese banker with a thick accent using New York slang. "When Trump tried to renegotiate the national debt, we almost got royally screwed. If it weren't for the bond markets going berserk, you would have gotten away with it. We're not giving you another shot at it. And since you started that trade war with the increased tariffs, it became politically impossible to do anything to help you guys out."

"Yeah," spoke up the Citigroup CEO, "but you got even with your tariffs on our stuff. And besides, our tariffs put half the Walmart stores in the country out of business. Doesn't that make us even? I tell you what, if you need collateral before you bail us out, how about California. We can get rid of a whole state of Democrats, all those Hollywood liberals and snotty Silicon Valley hotshots."

"Hey," Bank of America said, "we're in California. Why don't we give them New York, where Citibank is?"

"See," the Chinese banker said, "you can't even agree on this when your whole economy is on the rocks. This Trump Depression has got you at each other's throats."

"The Trump Depression!" shouted Trump. "What are they talking about? The economy was going great when I took office."

"Yes," said the spirit, "and for a while after. Obama left you a strong and growing economy, and your tax breaks gave a boost for a while. Things looked great. Then the expansion turned into a bubble after you deregulated everything you could. Then things started slowing down once the common folk, you know, the working class voters who put you into office, ran out of money and credit. The recession started. The billionaires had plenty, but nobody else did. The housing market crashed again, then the credit card market and the banks that depended on them, then every coastal community from Mar-A-Lago to Maine and the economies that depended on them. The recession really deepened. Then, of course, the wars."

"Wait!" Trump cried out. "This is too much at once. I don't understand how this could have gone wrong."

The spirit was patient, and spoke to Trump like he was an elementary school child who didn't study his history lessons. "Okay, we'll take it one at a time. When you and Congress weakened the Dodd-Frank reforms, the financial markets started speculating again. When you weakened Elizabeth Warren's consumer agency, the credit card companies went wild with over-expansion. People ran out of money to keep up with the debt, and that started it."

"Well, I guess that was to be expected," admitted Trump.

"You didn't expect it," pointed out the spirit.

"And the coastal problems?"

"Oh, that was a little more of a surprise. Remember that global warming phenomenon that you said was a myth? Well, that myth produced a few killer hurricanes. First came Hurricane Donald. The weather people have an ironic sense of humor when naming these things. It hit every community from Key West to North Carolina. There were about $120 billion in damages, a record. It was huge, believe me."

Trump had gotten used to the spirits throwing his words back at him, so he shrugged it off this time.

"Well, if that was the record, at least it didn't get worse. What about the rest of the coast?" he asked.

She shook her head. "It did get worse. A big hurricane from the South was joined by a big storm from the Northwest. It was a combination a lot like Superstorm Sandy. This one they named Hurricane Ivanka. They were still at it with the names, I guess. It hit from North Carolina to Massachusetts. There was tremendous damage to individual communities all along the coast, about $150 billion. But the worst damage was to the two rail tunnels between New Jersey and New York. One was knocked out completely, and the other partially. A third tunnel—you know, the one that Chris Christie cancelled—would have come in handy, but its replacement wasn't done yet. Transportation all up and down the East Coast was crippled."

"But wasn't there government money to help out?" Trump asked.

"What money? Donald had drained FEMA and all the other federal programs, and even required more, which the Congress quickly gave. When the Northeast was hit, there were no funds left, and Congress refused to allocate anything for quite a while. They figured that these were mostly Democratic states, so they couldn't resist the opportunity to stick it to them," said the spirit.

"They were getting back at their enemies," said Trump.

"Yes, I wonder where they picked up that philosophy? But revenge came at a price. When the economy of the Northeast tanked, it took a large part of the US economy with it. The recession got much worse."

"Well, at least they were able to blame the Democrats," said Trump.

"No, not this time. The behavior of the Republicans was so obvious, outrageous, and economically damaging that everyone was enraged. The financial community was mad about the effects on the economy and stock market. Voters throughout the area revolted. The Dems took both houses of the Pennsylvania legislature. Even gerrymandering couldn't save them. So, even the revenge thing didn't work too well."

"And what about these wars you mentioned?" asked Trump.

"That's our next stop. Hold my arm, and no funny business. I see how you're looking at my robes."

"Old habits," said Trump with a shrug of the shoulders.

They were flying again, out of Wall Street, down the East River, the Upper Bay and Lower Bay until they reached the Veterans Affairs Hospital in Bay Ridge in Brooklyn. He was proud to see that it had been renamed the Donald J. Trump Memorial Hospital, but wondered about the word *Memorial*. He also wondered why there was a big Hospital Corporation of America sign on top of the building.

They came in through one of the general medical wards, possibly the geriatrics unit because most of the veterans there were old and frail. Some were on oxygen, some IVs, and some were just sitting around the dayroom. Then they went into the rehabilitation unit. Here almost everyone was young, and there were both men and women. Some were missing arms, some legs, some had large bandages around their heads, and many were in the middle of physical therapy sessions.

"Which war are these soldiers from?" asked Trump.

"Well, some people call it the Third Gulf War, and some people call it Trump's War."

"My war? I wouldn't go out and start a war, would I?" asked Trump.

"No, you wouldn't. But you nominated lots of hard-line people to high levels in the military, and they were just itching for a war, especially with Iran."

"How did it start?"

"The hard-liners you appointed decided that they weren't going to take any crap from Iran, so they started a little game of chicken with them. US destroyers would go up to the limits of international waters, in the Strait of Hormuz, just where Iranian territory started, and then back off. The Iranians would send out small boats to check on the destroyers, and show they weren't going to be pushed around, but backing off at the last minute before they reached international waters. This went on for a while. One day, one of the Iranian boats went too far and was in international water with a US destroyer. The US destroyer cut them off."

"So, it shouldn't be a problem in international waters, should it?" asked Trump.

"It shouldn't, except that the Iranian boat commander used to be a New York City cab driver, and when he was cut off he gave the finger to the US ship."

"Yeah, I can see that," said Trump.

"Well, the US commander saw it, too. Do you remember that speech you gave when you said that if anyone makes a rude gesture to our military forces they should be shot out of the water?"

"I didn't mean it literally."

"The US commander thought you did, and he shot that Iranian boat out of the water, just the way he thought you wanted it."

"Really? Really, that was just a piece of rhetoric. I didn't mean it literally!" pleaded Trump.

"Too late," said the spirit. "The Iranians shot a bunch of missiles at the US ships, and the US ships shot a bunch of missiles at the Iranian shore batteries. Other US ships, including a carrier, immediately moved closer to the strait. The next day a few dozen Iranian ships of various sizes came out to meet the Americans. But it was only for show, and when they got too close and thought they would get fired on they turned back."

"Problem solved?" asked Trump.

"No, because two of the largest Iranian ships didn't turn back but kept coming. When they were within range, they were both shot at and sunk."

"Why didn't they take the warning like the other ships? Wouldn't they expect to be attacked?" asked Trump.

"No, they didn't expect to be shot, because they weren't Iranian ships. They were oil tankers. One was from Iraq, and one from a large Saudi refinery. They didn't expect to be attacked, and they weren't even in communication with the US ships. The US commander sent out drones but in the lousy rainy weather they couldn't confirm the tankers' identity before they became a threat, and were sunk."

Trump was really nervous when he asked his next question. "What did I do?"

"You punted. You said you would not second-guess the commanders in the field, and so the game of chicken continued. All oil traffic in the Persian Gulf stopped, and that's 20 percent of the world's total. The whole lower Persian Gulf was covered with oil. A little got out overland through Saudi Arabia, Iraq, and Syria, and the Iranians got theirs out through Pakistan, Turkey, Azerbaijan, and Turkmenistan."

Trump was a little confused. "We were talking about the Trump Depression. What did this have to do with it?"

"The price of oil went from thirty dollars a barrel to almost a hundred, especially when the speculators started to get involved. Gasoline prices in the US went from two dollars to over four. The economy was hurt, a lot, except of course for the oil companies who made a bundle. Then, there was a terrorist attack, and sinking, of an oil tanker over in the Mediterranean, insurance rates went sky high, and oil transport slowed down all over the world. A barrel went to two hundred, and gas prices in the US to six dollars. The economy really slowed."

"Did ISIS do that? I knew Obama couldn't stop them," said Trump.

The spirit was a little irritated. "No, it wasn't ISIS, and will you please stop blaming everything on Obama? You're not on the campaign trail now, and there's no excuse. Actually the US, Iraq, and Kurds wiped out ISIS in Iraq and Assad, the Russians, and Turkey destroyed them in Syria, along with the anti-Assad groups. It was a new group called Jihad21 that was founded after ISIS collapsed."

"Where did they come from?"

"Newark, New Jersey. A Muslim man there started it because he thought the US was waging a war against Islam, and not just Iran. He ended up in the Pakistani tribal areas and recruited his followers by Internet."

"See," said Trump, "you can't let Muslims into the US—they can't be trusted."

"He was born in Newark, as were his parents. He did it out of religion or ethnic identity or something like that. He worked in a Century 21 real estate office, and he thought it was such a wonderfully concise trademark that he adapted it for his group. You know, Jihad in the 21st Century," said the spirit.

"How could he recruit everyone over the Internet?" asked Trump.

"You helped him. He used to make promotional videos for his job and was good at putting together short, to-the-point, marketing messages. When he started Jihad21 he made short videos with clips of you and your various supporters, especially the military men, saying terrible things about Islam and Muslims. There were a ton of clips. It wasn't hard to convince lots of young people that the US hated Islam. Would you like to see some of the videos?"

"No, please, give me a break. I feel bad enough about this, you know, taking my comments out of context, or literally when I mean them rhetorically," said Trump.

"All right, I'll give you a break. Follow me," the spirit said as they floated through the medical ward. "Here are the patients with traumatic head injuries. These are some of the saddest cases. Even if they survive and do okay in rehab, many of them won't be anywhere near their prior level of functioning. Let's take a look."

Again, Trump hesitated. "It won't do me any good to see this. I get the point. It's all my fault for stoking confrontation without thinking it through."

"All right, another break. But this is the last one. Come," said the spirit, "let's see something a little less bloody."

They went down the hall a bit and came to the nurses' station. Some of the nurses were on computers in the front of the room, but in the back there were two people on the telephones. One was a doctor, and one a social worker.

The young doctor was talking into the telephone in an increasingly agitated manner. He finally slammed it down and turned to the social worker. "These insurance forms are crazy. This patient has been getting rehab for only three months for severe TBI and they want me to fill out a six-page form just to continue it. How much time do they think I have?"

The older social worker was sympathetic, but couldn't help much. "This company isn't much better. The doc ordered an MRI and the company wants justification as to why we're not doing an X-ray instead. Do any of these companies know what they're doing? Things were so much easier before privatization—one set of rules and what we ordered we got. Simple."

Trump was puzzled. "Why are they talking about insurance companies? This is the VA—there aren't any insurance companies here. This is the kind of thing those nurses were complaining about before, over in the nursing home."

The spirit smiled and corrected him. "There weren't any insurance companies here until your allies in Congress manipulated the budget to privatize the system. Remember how you said that the single-payer system works in other countries, so it should work here?"

"Yeah, I remember, and I got a lot of flak for it, too," said Trump.

"Actually, it works well here, too, or at least it did. This system was pretty close to a single-payer system, at least for the vets who got in. In case you hadn't noticed, your party hates single-payer systems. If something can't make a profit for a private company, it shouldn't exist. When Bernie Sanders wanted to increase VA funding years ago, the Republicans in Congress killed it. When the scandals hit, and funding became necessary, the Republicans linked it to options like going to outside doctors. Outside doctors eventually led to outside insurance companies, and when they balked they got big government subsidies. So, if you underfund a government program and subsidize the private sector, eventually the private sector has everything. That's why this hospital, and others around the country, were turned over to a private company, the Hospital Corporation of America, and others like it. There is no more VA system."

"What happens to the vets? Are they taken care of?" asked Trump.

"If they pick the right company, they do okay. If they pick the wrong one, they deteriorate and die. Congress did this, and either you didn't know what they were doing or you just went along. That's why HCA has its name on top of this building."

"That's a pretty cold-blooded way of looking at it. By the way, why is this place called the Donald J. Trump Memorial Hospital? *Memorial?*" asked Trump.

She shrugged. "I'm a spirit—we're all cold blooded. Besides, it's the truth. I'll answer your other question in time. Meanwhile, the only good thing is that the number of new vets is slowly going down. As the war heated up, the Republicans in Congress tried to have a resolution to give you unlimited authority to expand the war into nearby areas. The Dems referred to it as the Persian Gulf Resolution, you know, like the Tonkin Gulf Resolution that helped touch off the Vietnam War. You remember that war, it's the one you got out of because of the foot injury."

"A heel spur."

"Yes, of course, a heel spur." She knew very well what kept him out of the war, but couldn't resist needling him.

"As casualties kept coming in from those raids on the Iranian coastline, the occupation of some of their oil fields, and fighting with the Shiite militias in Iraq, the public turned against the war. That's when they nicknamed it Trump's War. When the Republicans started to lose House and Senate seats, along with a lot of state positions, treaties were negotiated and everything cooled down. There were still operations against Jihad21 wherever you could find them, but total casualties went down. Oh, except for one unusual one: Vladimir Putin."

Trump was shocked. "What did this have to do with Putin?"

"When oil prices skyrocketed from the war, Russia was rolling in money. He had a flat screen installed in his main meeting room and became obsessed with watching the prices per barrel go up and up. As the price of oil kept rising, he became more and more giddy with joy. When it hit 200 dollars a barrel, he started to laugh so much that he went into convulsions and dropped dead. The Russian doctors said they had never seen someone actually die laughing, but that's what happened. At least he was happy at the end."

"Well, good for him," said Trump dourly.

"By the way, when oil hit 200 a barrel, gas prices in the US hit six dollars a gallon. That's why they call this the Trump Depression. Enough of this, even I'm getting depressed," said the spirit as she cautiously took his arm. They were off again.

They flew down the coast of Brooklyn and passed the MCU stadium, on the site of the old Steeplechase Park. They slowed down to see what was happening. There was a massive demonstration going on. The stadium had a big banner across the top that said "Make America White Again" with lettering underneath that said "American Bund."

Trump was shocked. "How could they do that? That's outrageous."

"Oh, yes, outrage is what they want. Everyone in Brooklyn, from citizens to politicians to police, were against this event. To have neo-Nazis in Brooklyn was literally asking for trouble. But they took their case to the

Supreme Court, your Supreme Court, and they got a court order requiring the stadium to rent to them. They want a confrontation. The people around here are so outraged that this massive demonstration resulted. But the alt-right, Neos, and racists wanted a confrontation with the minorities. They already have people working on videos that they will post or sell to their supporters showing how white people who are sticking up for their rights are attacked by non-whites. They love this confrontation stuff."

"I never wanted their support," said Trump.

"You never publicly accepted their support. As for not wanting it, that would be a lot more convincing if you hadn't appointed some of them to government positions," said the spirit.

"My dad already lectured me on this. I think we can move on. Wait a minute, there's something I want to check out first."

This time, he led the spirit a few blocks away to where he saw the homeless Trump Tower South sign. The homeless encampment had become massive. There were small shacks with men, women, and even children trying to huddle inside. There was another Christmas tree over the camp, like before, but he didn't see anyone giving away gifts, and he didn't recognize any of the people he saw earlier.

"The people who were here before, are they still around?" he asked.

"This scene is years after your last one here. With the gross national product down 10 percent and the unemployment rate up to 15 percent—the official unemployment rate, that is—there is a lot of poverty around now, and a lot of these camps all over. Most are called Trumpvilles, or some similar name. And the poverty rate, which was 14.5 percent when you took over is now over 20 percent, another reason this is called—"

"I know, the Trump Depression. About those people . . .?"

She shook her head sadly. "Oh, yes. One, the women with the donuts, got into an assisted living designed for homeless people with mental illness. New York is one state that still uses its Medicaid money for things like that. Another woman took your advice and went to a homeless shelter. She got into an argument with another woman, got stabbed, and died in the Coney Island Hospital ICU.

"The guy who brought the coffee was caught shoplifting a bunch of times. He was stealing some bread. He's in Rikers Island Prison right now because he can't make a thousand dollar bail. He's been there a few months, I think."

Trump was astonished. "A few months in jail because he can't make a thousand dollar bail? What sense does that make? Aren't there any programs to help people like that? I thought I remembered one like that up in the Bronx."

"Aren't you sure those programs aren't just bull? Those guys who came to you for a donation tonight were raising money for a whole bunch of programs like that, including the one up in the Bronx. And you said what?" needled the spirit.

"Bull. I said bull." He looked at the homeless people all around him. "Have we seen enough in Brooklyn? My hometown is making me sick to my stomach."

"Is it your hometown that's making you sick, or is it yourself?" asked the spirit.

"What's the guy's name? Maybe I can help," said Trump.

"Jean Valjean," said the spirit.

"What!?" shouted Trump.

"No, only kidding. I never get tired of that Jean Valjean joke when I'm on a project like this. It lightens the mood, at least for me. And, no, we have one more stop in Brooklyn."

They continued to fly down the Brooklyn coast until they came to an old housing project.

"I recognize this place. This is one of the government low-income projects my dad built," said Trump.

Without saying a word, the spirit led him up a stairway and through a doorway into a small apartment. There was a woman sitting in front of a table stacked with papers and legal documents. They floated around in front of her until Trump recognized her. It was Ivanka, his daughter.

"What is she doing here? She should be managing one of my casinos, at least, not a public housing project," said Trump.

"She doesn't manage this place . . . she lives here," the spirit calmly announced.

Trump was angry. "No, she doesn't. This is one of those spirit-world tricks, and I'm getting a little tired of them. Who is this woman, really, and why are we here?"

The spirit was still calm in spite of Trump's anger. "I don't expect you to believe this, until I explain how it happened. You see, when you became president, you turned over all your properties to your kids. It avoided conflict of interest accusations against you, and gave them the properties they would eventually be getting anyway. Besides, your kids are the only people you can trust. Everything else being equal, this should have worked out well. But everything else wasn't equal. You were immune from attack, but your kids weren't. Every enemy you ever had, every enemy you made during your terms—"

"Terms? Did you say terms as in plural?" asked an energized Trump.

"Oops, there I go again. Never mind what I said about you. Your daughter is sitting right in front of you with a kitchen table full of problems. Focus, Mr. Trump, focus. Where was I? Oh, yes, not only were your enemies after you, but others who had learned your tricks and were about to use them against your interests and family, if not against you personally, just in order to make a financial killing. You bragged about your wealth so much that everybody in the world, literally the world, who had a good lawyer thought they could cash in. Some felt they were justified, and some just wanted a payout. In either case, your kids became your proxy targets."

"Even the Mafia doesn't go after families," Trump said, shocked.

"We're not talking about those Mafia softies. We're talking about real estate and politics. These are the barracudas out there, and they play for much bigger stakes then a mobster shaking down some construction project for a cement contract."

"Don't remind me," said Trump, holding his head.

Just then, the phone rang and Ivanka picked it up. When he heard her voice he was a little more convinced it really was her. "Hi, how are things going with the lawsuits? Uh-huh, uh-huh."

Trump strained to hear what was being said on the other end, but couldn't.

Ivanka continued. "All right, I know the Cuban exiles are all after us because they can't get the Cuban government. If only my dad's Supreme Court hadn't overturned that law the Republicans passed during the Obama years. Then they could go straight after them. But, I guess with all the suits against the US they had to overturn it just to protect our government. But where does that leave me? Just because I do business with them . . . oh, ok, they go after the deep pockets wherever they can get them. I'll tell you, though, these pockets aren't so deep anymore. That's why we have to pay your fees on a contingency from our countersuits, if we win them. Please win a few of those cases, though, so I can move out of here. I can't believe my grandfather built such dumpy apartments. They even got worse after Hurricane Ivanka. Yeah, I know. Ivanka's apartment damaged by Hurricane Ivanka. Real ironic. Anyway, we'll talk again next week unless there's something new. Bye."

"So she got the Guantanamo casino deal? I thought that would be such a moneymaker," Trump said, shaking his head in disbelief.

The phone rang again, and Ivanka picked it up. "Oh, Arabella, it's so good to hear from you. Why so late . . . what's up? Uh-huh, uh-huh. Don't say those things about your stepmother, it won't do any good. I was able to eat kosher, so can you. I don't care if all the other kids are eating cheeseburgers, your house over there is kosher and that's all there is to it. I'll see you next weekend. Maybe we can find a place with fake cheese and turkey bacon. There's got to be someplace in Brooklyn that does that. That should be okay. Say hello to your brothers for me, but don't wake them up. Love you."

Trump was confused. "Why did she divorce that Kushner guy? I thought they were getting along so well? She even converted for him."

"She didn't divorce him, he divorced her. When you sent him over to Israel to do those peace negotiations, he met some really attractive Orthodox girl. You know, tanned, fit, and a lot younger than Ivanka. They saw each other every time he went over there. Then she moved here, up to Williamsburg I think, and they saw each other on the sly."

Trump was furious. "What nerve! That little putz marries a beautiful woman in a rich family, gets three kids from her while she helps him with his business with all sorts of connections, and then cheats on her with a younger woman. She even converted! Damn him to hell! Really, you're a spirit, can't you damn him?"

The spirit would have none of it. "Does that story remind you of any other family situation?"

Trump stopped short, realized what she was saying, and tried to defend himself. "Ivana was a lot older when we broke up, and we had years of problems before that. It's not the same thing."

Again, the spirit wouldn't yield. "A lot older? Remember, Mr. Trump, we've travelled ahead in time. Take a good look at your daughter."

Trump looked more closely. The spirit was right. Ivanka was older and fortyish, just like Ivana when they divorced. The situations weren't completely alike, but they were pretty close. For once, Trump shut up.

But, that didn't last long. "The boys, how are the boys doing?"

"Barron is in Wharton, and Eric and Donald Junior both moved up to the Bronx with their families. They got two adjacent, old brownstones and fixed them up. They're gorgeous. Let's go up and see them."

Trump objected. "The Bronx! I'm not going up to the Bronx, I don't care who's up there. Can't you do some spirit magic and bring them down here? Well, anyway, we've been trying to gentrify the Bronx for decades. Is that what they're doing?"

"Not exactly. They've been hit by lawsuits also. The houses were really cheap, next to each other, and easy to fix up. Too bad you don't want to visit, you'd be impressed."

"What happened?" asked Trump.

"Well, Eric's story is shorter. He went into business with Soros, like you planned. Soros had a lot of political connections, and Eric had a lot of money, or at least was able to borrow a lot of money. But when it was close to completion, Soros and all his connections backed out. He convinced the politicians that foreign influence was getting too great. And, with Donald Junior's Russian deals, he convinced the politicians that it was unpatriotic to do dealings with anyone who might be connected to the Russians, however indirect. He even had a slogan—Make Hungary Great Again."

"Catchy. I wonder where he got it," Trump said with cold sarcasm in his voice.

The spirit continued. "Soros got plenty of government funding after that and got his casino and resort up and running. Eric got sued by every creditor and many of his stockholders. He's up to his neck in court right now."

"I'm a little afraid to ask. How's Donald Junior doing?"

"He's doing the same as Eric, except fourfold."

Trump was incredulous. "He lost all four casinos? How?"

"He was screwed by Putin, just before he died. The casino in Sochi was condemned and given to some oligarch cousin of his who fixed it and opened it under his own name. The casinos in Moscow and St. Petersburg were undermined the same way, and given to two political supporters of Putin."

Shaking his head, Trump asked, "Vladivostok? What happened to that dump in Vladivostok? I thought that one was going well."

"After you finished off the Trans-Pacific Partnership it was open season out there. Everyone was making deals. Your place was good, and your offer was solid, but when Sheldon Adelson made a much better offer, they dumped yours, I mean your son's, and gave it to him."

"What traitors!" shouted Trump. "And all the things I did for Putin. If it weren't for me, that whole country would still be an economic disaster. Okay, I did some of these things accidentally, but still it helped him a lot."

The spirit had a slight smile on her face when she said, "Putin couldn't help but be Putin. Did you ever hear the joke about the scorpion and the frog? The scorpion was just being a scorpion, and Putin was just being Putin."

Trump was still mad. "Adelson has all the money in the world. What's the matter with these rich old guys who have more money than they need and still they go after more?"

The spirit had a fake quizzical look on her face when she answered with, "Yes, what is the matter with these old guys who have everything and still want more? What is it?"

Trump calmed down. "Well, did they at least get some money from selling the property, or selling the international options and contracts?"

"Yes, your company did get something. But when you borrow billions and get back hundreds of millions at a fire sale, that still leaves you deeply in the hole. There was no way to pay off everyone, and the company got sued like crazy. As I said, he had the problems of Eric, and even Ivanka, but just four times as much. Oh, the Russians did offer something in Sevastopol, but nobody, not even Donald Junior, would touch that with the legal status of Crimea up in the air."

"Tiffany. Please tell me she's okay," Trump pleaded.

"She's doing fine. She's back in California, either Venice Beach or Marina del Ray. She kept a low profile and completely backed out of any real estate wheeling and dealing, at least so far. California sun can sometimes mellow you out fantastically."

"She couldn't live in Malibu or Pacific Palisades?" Trump asked.

"She's fine, let her be," lectured the spirit.

Trump was exhausted from all of this. "You know, spirit, you're asking a lot. I'm supposed to change all the values I've had my whole life—the getting even, the never trusting, the never being satisfied with what I have—and do it in one night. I'm also supposed to learn the spirit of Christmas and be generous and start having group hugs. You know what a germaphobe I am. I don't know if I can do it. Maybe we should just hook up the chains and stuff right now. I did the best I could at the time with the training and values I had. I don't regret the things I did."

"You don't regret the things you did? Maybe our next few stops will make you think otherwise," said the spirit with a very cold look in her eyes.

In an instant they were in another room. It was familiar to Trump. This was the Rodriguez home. It was dark, but with enough light that he could see Maria lying on the couch. Juan Junior wasn't around, nor were his inhalers. I have a bad feeling about this, Trump thought.

"Where is everybody?" he asked.

There was tension in the spirit's voice as she spoke, almost harshly. "Juan Senior is up in Tallahassee. The court case against your company is still going on, and it was bumped up to some state court up in the capital. Carmen is out waitressing. Their finances are still very poor, and she takes all the shifts she can get."

"And Junior?"

Her voice became harsher. "You remember how you said you were going to repeal Obamacare? Well, you were successful. At first there was a patchwork of programs to replace it, but none worked very well and the number of uninsured people rose by almost twenty million. Then Ryan got his dream package passed, which turned Medicaid into a block program. Each state would get a large block of money almost equal to their Medicaid budget, and they would spend it as they decided. States' rights won out— oh, I mean, federalism. *States' rights* has such bad connotations, don't you think?"

Trump was cautious when he asked, "So did the states accept these Medicaid programs, or give the Feds a hard time like they did with Obamacare?"

"Well, since this was coming from a Republican Congress and Republican president, all the objections that had been used against Obamacare disappeared. But the Medicaid blocks were looted as soon as they got to the states. First, they were inadequate since the theory was that the states were so efficient they wouldn't need as much money. Then the states started diverting the money to other things. Some went to golf courses and sports stadiums on the grounds that they encouraged exercise, which encouraged health. Other money went to prisons, which had a little bit of medical care at least, but the funds were used also for general construction and maintenance. Medicaid shrunk and shrunk, and the requirements became so strict that millions who would have qualified before were kicked off."

"But what about Junior?" Trump asked, now getting very nervous.

"The Rodriguez family owns their home, and they have a car. Both things were held against them. When they needed care, they ended up in a nearby emergency room."

"So, they could get care. Junior's okay then, wherever he is," said Trump, looking around the room for any signs of him.

"Asthma is a bad disease when it's not properly treated. When you go from emergency visit to emergency visit it gets worse and worse, and the medications cost a fortune. You have to prevent the attacks in the first

place, and for that you need a family doctor, or nurse practitioner, or somebody. And, you need the money to buy the meds."

Trump stood there, silently.

"You're not asking any more questions. Why not?" she said with
fake sweetness.

"Because I know the answer," he said with uncharacteristic sadness,
and maybe even a little regret. Yes, the regret was starting to kick in as the
significance of his decisions became unavoidable.

The sweetness was done. "Damn right, you know the answer! And you
know what else? He didn't die comfortably. He was on a ventilator in inten-
sive care for a week. Toward the end they had to put him in a medically
induced coma so he wouldn't try and get out of bed, or pull out his IV line,
or pull out the tube down his throat, or pull out the tube in his dick. How
would you like to spend the last week of your life with a tube in your dick?"

Trump was shaken. Even his father's lecture and wailing didn't get to
him like this did. "I didn't mean for that kid to die! Are you going to hold
me responsible for every death in this country?"

The spirit calmed down a bit and said, "No, you didn't mean for him
to die and you're not responsible for every death in this country. But each
decision you make pushes the odds a little further against them. And what
you don't do those fanatics in Congress will if you let them and forget
where your Veto pen is."

He was quiet for a while. Then he heard a moan from Maria.

"Mama," she said softly.

Trump looked over and asked the spirit, "Is she okay? She looks sick."

"She is sick. Remember when I told you about the family losing
Obamacare and the Medicaid? Well, there's a few more things they lost.
When you put those anti-abortion judges on the court and they overturned
Roe v. Wade, they didn't stop there. Because there was no right to privacy,
which is how they justified killing *Roe v. Wade*, then there wouldn't be

any for *Griswold v. Connecticut*, which guaranteed a right to birth control information. Not abortion, birth control."

"Anybody can get birth control, that couldn't be a problem," he said.

"It was when they started to reinstate the Comstock laws."

"The Comstock laws?"

A weary look came over the face of the spirit. "They prevented birth control information or devices from going through the US mail. They prevented a lot of people from getting birth control material, at least cheaply and efficiently."

"So what does this have to do with Maria?" he asked.

He looked over at her, covered in a light white blanket as she slept. "Mama," she said softly.

"Let me take you through this quickly, as we don't have much time left. After *Roe* was overturned, the Congress decided to give fetuses, or embryos, or unborn babies, depending on what terms you use, civil rights."

"That sounded only fair, and I signed it," Trump said, not sure where this was going.

"And do you remember the law you signed saying that women who get abortions should be punished? With this civil rights law, women could be prosecuted."

"What's the sense of having a law if you don't enforce it?" he asked.

"Well, the states, including Florida, took it further. They began charging mothers with murder if they had abortions, and they began enforcing that law any time a local district attorney wanted to make a name for himself or herself. Women started going to jail for abortions."

"Overturning *Roe v. Wade* was supposed to stop a lot of those abortions."

The spirit continued her lecture. "It stopped a constitutional right to a safe abortion. It didn't ban abortion. Women who want abortions have been doing so since time began, and will continue to do so no matter what.

Evangelical women have abortions. Catholics have abortions. It was even in the Hippocratic oath two and a half thousand years ago. He didn't care about safe abortions any more than Congress does, or those fanatics you appointed to the Supreme Court. Women with a little money could perhaps travel to another state where access to someone who would perform abortions could be found, but then they risked murder charges when they returned home. Poor women, like Maria, had no choice."

He looked at Maria and finally got the point of the spirit's ranting. "You mean she got pregnant?"

"Yes!"

"And she had an abortion?"

"Yes!"

"But where? It's banned here."

"She did it herself!" and the spirit pointed over to the kitchen table. On it was a long, thin file that her father used for some of his wood carving, and a bottle of rubbing alcohol next to it for sterilization. There was blood on the file.

"We've got to get her to a hospital," he said as he instinctively reached for the cell phone on the other side of the room. When his spirit hand went through the table, he was reminded of his powerlessness.

"Mama . . . ."

He looked at her again and pointed to her blanket. There was a small red dot in the middle of it. She was sweating profusely.

Maria was no relative of his, and he had never met her except during tonight's travels, but her well-being was the only thing in the world he was focusing on right now.

"Why didn't she go to the hospital?" he asked in a more panicked voice.

"She did," responded the spirit coldly. "She couldn't tell them she tried to abort a fetus, she would have gone to jail. She couldn't tell them she was having a miscarriage or heavy menstrual period since the state requires emergency rooms to notify them of all such cases. She would have gone to jail anyway when they examined her closely and found the signs of an abortion. They gave her a prescription for some antibiotics, which she was going to get filled tomorrow after she borrowed some money to pay for it. This hospital was a private one, belonging to a for-profit chain of hospitals. They didn't want to admit her for observation because she didn't have insurance, but they did give her the address of the county hospital, miles away, and of a local storefront clinic that would open in the morning."

He looked over at her and saw the red dot bloom larger, maybe the size of a teacup saucer. He bent over and looked at her closely and remembered that she looked like Ivanka, although with the malaise and sweating it was less apparent.

Trump was starting to talk to himself, and began ranting just a bit. "Why didn't she tell her father? No, that's right, he was in Tallahassee. Why didn't she tell her mother?"

"Because that would make her an accessory to murder. She protected her mother, that's why," said the spirit. "And now she's septic and bleeding out."

At the next "Mama," Trump jumped and tried to look away.

"Don't you dare look away!" said the spirit in an even colder and harsher voice.

The red area was as big as a soup bowl now.

"I didn't want things like this to happen. I'm not responsible for this," he said desperately.

"Yes, you didn't want this to happen, but it's happening all over the country now anyway, and you *are* responsible. Who appointed those judges to the court that were against legal, safe, medical abortions, and even against birth control availability? Who overturned Obamacare without a viable alternative? Who let the Congress gut Medicaid, and allowed the states to gut it even more at the first chance they got? Who made abortion a little bit illegal and then stood by when the states made it very, very illegal? Who did all that? Didn't you *ever* think about the consequences of your actions?"

He looked over at Maria. The red dot was as large as a dinner plate, but she was quiet and had stopped sweating. He was reassured for a second.

"The worst is over. She's quiet now," he calmly said.

"Yes, the worst is over. She's dead." There were tears rolling down her eyes, another emotion he never associated with ghosts. The spirit looked down at the dead Maria, and her face was calm and mournful as the face of Mary in Michelangelo's *Pieta* as she looked down on the body of the dead Christ. He suddenly remembered this was Christmas Eve, or maybe Christmas Day by now.

He also remembered something else he had said, in this very room, earlier in the evening. But he dared not say it out loud. Instead, the spirit did. "I know what you're thinking. Maybe she shouldn't have gotten pregnant. And maybe this poor kid should have just had a baby in a family that was struggling every day. And maybe her father shouldn't have done business with you. And maybe they shouldn't have come to the US in the first place. There are a lot of maybes in this situation. Here's another. Maybe you shouldn't have done some of those things you did, without thinking."

"I've never seen death up close like this," he whispered.

"You're going to see it a lot closer in a few minutes," she warned, and they were off again.

They were in a cold, misty, dark area. After a few seconds he realized they were in a graveyard. He turned to the spirit and asked, "Why are we here?" But this time, the spirit didn't speak, she just pointed up the side of the hill, and began to walk in that direction. He followed. After a little while they came to one solitary gravestone separated from the rest, with two National Park Service armed guards standing next to it. The coldest chill he had ever felt ran up his spine. The spirit quietly pointed to the stone. This silence frightened him more than all the lectures, wailing, berating, and sights he had seen all night, except for what he saw during Maria's death.

He bent down to get a closer look at what he knew would be there. It was a beautiful, but plain and traditional granite headstone. On it, in gold, of course, were chiseled the words "Donald J. Trump, President of the United States, June 14, 1946 to—." He couldn't make out the final date. He rubbed it, but, of course, that didn't help as his hands went through the solid stone. He looked at the very bottom and saw a small inscription, which read "Donated by the grateful people of Russia for all that he has bestowed upon us." What was that doing there?

He stood up and faced the guards but jumped back in horror. Instead of the guards, there stood two ghosts. One was clearly his father, with his chain wrapped around his waist and with an expression on his face that was sadder than any Trump had ever seen during his life or earlier this evening. The ghost slowly looked to the other ghost who Trump didn't recognize. It was an old man, though not as old as his father. He looked closer and realized who it was. It was an older, sadder Donald Trump, sadder than he had ever seen himself in life. Trump quickly looked on the ground and saw a tremendous chain of links, books, papers, campaign banners, and cell phones. When he didn't see the chain wrapped around his waist or his neck he started to search frantically, thinking of the only likely alternative attachment point.

But, the spirit stepped in front of him and pointed down the hill. As desperate as he was to examine his eternal fate in whatever detail he could, he knew he couldn't disobey the spirit. He turned and slowly walked down the hill, turning around only once to see that the guards had reappeared and the ghosts vanished. He walked down the hill, quietly thinking about the events of the night, including his tombstone. He had always thought he would have something a little more elaborate. The tombstones of Nixon and Johnson were pretty plain, but Reagan at least had a little wall with some of his quotations engraved around it.

As he got to the bottom of the hill, he saw a large crowd. There were Park Service Guards, a lot of local police, a bunch of civilians in handcuffs being put into police vans, and others being put into ambulances. On the ground were three bodies covered in white sheets. The sheets reminded Trump of Maria's blanket, and a deep shudder went through him. He walked over to some of the guards and overheard their conversation, keeping an eye on the spirit as if to ask for permission.

An older guard was talking. "Yes, I was here the first Trump day. It was really something. There were thousands of demonstrators, and they caught us completely off guard. Men, women, transgenders, every race, every age—it was a sight. We thought they were coming to praise him, but they were really here to curse him. They attacked us and then marched up the hill to the mausoleum. It was really beautiful, believe me. White marble, a lot of gold, some of Trump's sayings carved in a big wall that was in a semicircle behind the sarcophagus. It wouldn't be my taste in a tomb, but I guess it fit him well enough."

The younger guard asked, "How did they get it down?"

"Oh, they tore at it like wild animals. They used hammers, sledgehammers, picks, chisels, even bare hands. They really hated him. The local cops got here just as they were attacking the sarcophagus and drove them off. Only about a dozen killed that day, not the worst we've ever had. Since then every Trump Day, the 14th of every month, they come back. Sometimes it's a big crowd, sometimes small, sometimes violent, sometimes peaceful. Usually there are a mix of demonstrators, you know, depending on the issue. But sometimes they manage to keep it on one issue. One month it's global warming and justice for victims of Hurricane Ivanka, and the next it's the American-born children of deported illegals."

"How do they know to show up if there's a specific group?" asked the youngster.

"Tweets, of course, and a lot of other social media. Ironic, isn't it? He loved tweets so much, and now they're being used to organize against him even after he's dead. But you know what I never see here? His supporters. He had so many, almost a majority of the country . . . ."

Trump winced when he heard this fact quoted again. Even in death they won't let him forget it.

"But they all abandoned him. The evangelicals didn't show up, the Neos didn't show up, the mainstream Republicans didn't show up, even all those working-class guys didn't show up. His family always showed, but only on June 14th, his real birthday. His kids, grandkids, ex-wives, and even a few older women who may have been girlfriends, who knows? They didn't say, and I didn't ask, and don't you ask. We're here as guards, not paparazzi."

"I heard a lot of coal miners showed up once," said the youngster.

"That was on a protest day. Lots of coal miners. Tough guys, tough women. After they realized he wasn't going to bring the coal mine jobs back, and that Wikileak guy sent out hacked stuff showing he knew about it during his campaign and had lied to them, they turned on him like crazy."

"Today was a bad day, wasn't it?" the youngster asked.

"We knew it would be. The unemployment rate topped 15 percent last month, and the stock market just went below 10,000. We knew it would be bad, but to be honest, only three dead during the demonstrations isn't that bad."

The spirit motioned over to Trump, and pointed to one of the covered bodies on the ground. At first he couldn't see anything, but then a gust of wind came, maybe with the help of the spirit, and uncovered the body. It was Juan Rodriguez, a lot older and with a big bullet hole in his head. On his chest were two small cameos with pictures of Juan Junior and Maria, both smiling and beautiful. Why did he come there and risk his life? Didn't he still have a wife who would need comforting after the death of their two children? Trump then remembered what his father said about being hated. Those who hate you will do anything to bring you down, or even dishonor you after you're dead, regardless of the damage to themselves.

He turned to the spirit, not knowing what else to do. This time there were tears in his eyes. Real tears, not crocodile tears. The spirit reached out, but instead of touching his arm, she touched him on his chest, over his heart.

They were back in his room.

"I've got to change," said Trump to the spirit. "I don't know how, there's so much, but I have to. Those images from tonight, my dad, my decisions at Fordham, Trump Tower South, Putin laughing at me behind my back, my family ruined, those coal miners I double crossed, those bastards in Congress who used me, my desecrated grave, and—and—." Choking up made him unable to add "the Rodriguez family."

The spirit started to speak again. "These images are strong, because they demand a big challenge. They are to help you save your soul."

Trump added, almost as an afterthought, "And that silence at the cemetery had the desired dramatic effect also."

"It wasn't done for dramatic effect. It was done because there was really nothing I could say to add to what you saw. If your own grave and your own ghost don't get you to change, then there's nothing I could do."

"Yeah, a bunch of ghosts and banshees can't frighten you like your own ghost."

Without realizing it, again he had made a terrible mistake by speaking without thinking. By describing this beautiful woman before him as a banshee, even indirectly, he just set her off. He didn't consider that she had seen the same horrible scenes that he had and she was as broken up as he was. She snapped.

"Banshees! We give up one of the happiest days of the year to come here and help you save your black soul, and you call us banshees!"

He was shocked, but before he could apologize she screamed out again. "You want to see real banshees? I'll show you a friggin' banshee!"

With that, all the soft tissue on her angelic face vaporized, and only a horrible death skull was left. Her perfect white teeth were changed to bloody fangs. The cloak dropped from her body, and instead of seeing a voluptuous figure Trump saw a skeleton of only bones. Her hands and feet changed into claws, like hagravens in a computer game, and two large devil-type wings sprung out of her spine. She let out a screech like he had never heard before, and his spirit staggered back and fell into his body, quietly sleeping on the bed.

CHAPTER FIVE

When Trump woke the next morning, he was almost giddy with excitement. He had to get oriented first, so he sent out a tweet.

"What day is today?" he said in one of his briefest tweets ever. Most respondents assumed he was asking a rhetorical question, and they tweeted back with salutations and best wishes for Christmas Day. He was glad to see he hadn't missed a day, since the previous night's visits seemed to last forever. Then he noticed something on the return tweets. He went to his bedroom door and asked the Secret Service agents to call for their supervisor.

He came quickly. "Agent Joe Petrosino, at your service," the super straight agent said.

Trump's giddiness had calmed down to just plain enthusiasm by this point. "Agent Petrosino, I need an experienced hand for something. Have you been doing this long? Do you know the supervisors down at headquarters?"

"My family has been in the law enforcement business for over a century, and I have fifteen years myself with various Treasury Department positions," he said.

"So I can depend on you for something that must be done discreetly," Trump whispered.

"Eh, I'd take a bullet if I had to, although I'm not looking forward to it. And they don't call us the *Secret* service for nothing."

Both the agent's New York accent and New York sense of humor made him seem pretty trustworthy. Trump's rule of never trusting anyone would have to be suspended a little.

"You still monitor my tweets?"

"Yes, sir."

"And the return tweets?"

"Yes, sir."

"Well," said Trump, "look at this one. It ends in 'Heil Trump.' There are a few like that. These guys are dangerous. The white supremacists, neo-Nazis, Klansmen, alt-right, or whatever you want to call them have a violent streak that seems to be getting out of control. I want you to tell headquarters to monitor and then track everyone who sounds like they're in this faction. Hook up with the folks at the Southern Poverty Law Center if you have to. They have really good information. But, don't let on to what you're doing. Monitor but don't intercede if you can avoid it. I'll keep re-tweeting them now and then to draw more out. I'd rather have them out in the open than underground. Eventually they'll overplay their hands, but for now just monitor."

The agent was a little hesitant. "Some of these guys are high up in your administration, at least according to the papers and the ones you've announced so far. You want us to keep an eye on them, too?"

"Especially them," said Trump.

"But you've helped out these guys a lot, like Bannon. You still don't trust them?"

"Especially Bannon. I've helped them a lot, but they think they've helped me more. I have it on very solid and very high authority that these guys think I owe them. If I don't keep them happy, they'll turn on me in a second, including Bannon. And they won't be easy to keep happy."

The agent nodded. He was a history buff, and this reminded him of the Night of the Long Knives, when Hitler had a bloody purge of the Brown Shirts, who supported him, and eliminated them from his administration. He wasn't equating Trump with Hitler, it was only an analogy, but equating the alt-right with the Brown Shirts wasn't too far off the mark.

Trump was at his desk, holding a business card and making a telephone call. After a minute he turned to Petrosino. "I have to meet somebody a few blocks up Fifth Avenue. After that we can go to the heliport and make it down to Washington in time for this afternoon's White House reception. Let's go."

Trump and the contingent of agents barreled out of the apartment and onto the street. There weren't as many demonstrators as last night, but there were plenty of media people and onlookers who wanted a picture of him. This was just what he wanted, but not for the usual egotistical reasons.

After a short walk they entered the lobby of another fancy Fifth Avenue apartment house. Melchior Ebrahim was standing in the lobby waiting for him. "This really is a surprise," he said, "but thanks for coming. Have you changed your mind by any chance?"

Trump nodded. "Yes, I have, and I want to apologize for being such a jerk yesterday. Aren't there shelters, aren't there prisons. What was I thinking?"

"Apologize? You?" Melchior was clearly shocked.

"Not just apologize, but give you this check. I heard from a really good authority last night, after you left, and he said you do excellent work. Do you, by any chance, support that group in the Bronx that provides bail to poor people arrested for minor offenses?"

"Yes, we do. You heard about it?"

"Like I said, I had some really good information last night. Let's go outside and hand over the check in front of all those cameras and cell phone people. This will be on social media in seconds. You can use it, too, if you want, on your website and publicity work. I want you to hit up every developer, Wall Street guy, and hedge fund operator you can."

They walked outside the building, and Trump handed over the check as conspicuously as possible. Both Trump and Melchior were smiling broadly, and the picture was flashing around the Internet in a few seconds. What's more, Trump had a new warm feeling in him. He felt really good. They said good-bye, and Trump headed to the heliport.

In the helicopter he got another idea to assist him in his transformation. He took out his cell phone, looked up a number, and called. "I'm trying to get Senator Schumer. Chuck, is that you? This is Donald Trump. Oh, don't call me that, I'm not in office yet, still just a civilian. Sorry to call so early and on Christmas. Oh, that's right. So what will you be doing? A Chinese restaurant? Oh yeah, I know the place, and it's very good.

"But listen. I'm calling about something else, something very important. You know the people I'll be appointing, or considering appointing, to my cabinet and to advisory positions. Well, I've had a change of heart. These people are fanatics, lunatics, greed heads, idiots, and racists. The day after I'm inaugurated I'm going to ask most of them to resign, and start appointing an entirely new cabinet and staff.

"Chuck, are you still there? Iris, is he okay? Fainted? Gee, I'm sorry, I should have told him to be ready. Yes, put him back on. Chuck, you okay? Sorry for the shock.

I want a cabinet like Obama has, but further to the left and much more populist. I want someone with the populism of Bernie but the fire of Elizabeth Warren. No, I don't want those two specifically, you'll need all the help in the Senate you can get. But, someone like that. And for attorney general I don't want a pushover like Holder who didn't send anyone to jail. I want someone with the bloodlust of Giuliani but who's not a *gavone.* Maybe Lynch can stay on if she learns how to sharpen her knives a little."

He waited for a few seconds to hear Schumer's response, and then continued. "I want it to be a complete surprise, so they don't have time to respond. I need you to vet me a cabinet. Tell them that since you'll be the ranking Democrat in the Senate you'll need a staff of advisors. You can use anyone from past cabinets who've already been checked out. That will make it faster. Poor Hillary . . . yes, that's what I said, poor Hillary, jumped the gun and started looking at people, too, so maybe you can pick her brain. But don't tell her why, use the same cover story. This has to be a complete surprise, or my own party will pick me apart.

"Okay, we'll start meeting in the city. You know, the spirit of reconciliation and bi-partisanship and all that stuff will be our cover. But, no emails. I hate emails. And no tweets about this."

Trump was really pleased with himself. The part of him that was still the old Trump was enjoying the scheming and manipulation. Machiavelli himself would be proud. He felt bad that his dad didn't get a chance to introduce them to each other. Maybe later. The new Trump was feeling good because he was doing something that wasn't self-centered for a change.

He landed on the White House lawn and went into the reception room. His entire family was there, except for the ex-wives, of course. The Obamas were there, too, and everyone seemed to be getting along well. He went around and said hello to everyone, kissed his present wife and kids, stood for a few publicity shots, and had a bite to eat. The low-fat, non-alcoholic, organic eggnog was surprisingly good, and the veggies from Michelle's garden were excellent.

Then he managed to pull President Obama and Michelle over to the side, and started talking seriously.

"I've had a big change of heart concerning the direction of my administration," he said.

Cautiously, Obama asked, "What brought this on?"

"You wouldn't believe me if I told you. But the important thing is that there will be changes in the way I've been doing things, and changes in what I've been saying."

"Like what?" Obama asked, still cautious.

"I'm going to repeal Obamacare," said Trump.

"Yes, I know that," said Obama.

"I'm going to replace it with something better."

"I know that, too."

"I'm going to pass a single-payer healthcare bill and wipe out all the private insurance companies," said Trump proudly.

Obama was stunned, but incredulous. "How can you do that? I didn't even come close, even when Democrats still had the House. And your people hate the idea of a single-payer system."

"They won't be my people anymore."

He then outlined his plan for a surprise in his inaugural address and a staff purge the day afterward.

"The rest of your party will have a fit. What happens when they turn on you? What will you say?"

"I'll say, 'What did you expect? You knew what I was like when you voted for me' and refer them to the joke about the scorpion and the frog."

"Yes, I know the joke," said Obama.

Oblivious, and on a roll, Trump continued, "You see, there was this scorpion who wanted to cross a river, but couldn't swim."

"Yes, I know it," said Obama and Michelle simultaneously.

"So he asks a frog to take him over, but the frog says if he does that the scorpion will sting him and we'll—"

"Both die," said Obama.

"Both die," echoes Trump. "But the scorpion says, 'That doesn't make sense, because I'll die too.'"

Obama and Michelle rolled their eyes.

"So the frog says okay, and takes the scorpion to the middle of the river. The scorpion stings the frog, and as they're both going down the frog asks, 'Why did you do that?'"

Obama and Michelle were silent.

"And the scorpion says, 'Because I'm a scorpion.'"

"Yeah, that's a good joke," said Obama politely. "But that's your ethical defense, a scorpion is a scorpion and Trump is Trump. What about the practical part of getting it through Congress?"

Trump had an uncharacteristically wise and thoughtful expression on his face when he answered. "First, the Democrats have to stick together, with no Blue Dog Democrat defections. Pelosi has a track record of controlling her people, and I think Schumer will do the same. The Republicans are fractured. Some are my die-hard supporters, some are Tea Party people, and some are mainstream. My supporters are dependable. If I shot a guy in the middle of Fifth . . . oh, wait, you know that one. Anyway, the Tea Party people will support me when they hear the details."

"And the mainstream ones?" asked Obama, beginning to like this idea.

"I just crushed every mainstream Republican in the party during the primaries."

"All right," said Obama, "what are the details?"

Trump started, enthusiastically, "Every legal resident of the country goes into Medicare, we get rid of all the copayments, deductibles, exclusions like drugs and nursing homes, and increase payments for doctors. The Tea Party people hate government programs, but not the ones they benefit from. They'll be on board, and so will the doctors if we increase payments enough."

Obama thought for a minute. "But what about the insurance companies? This plan is a death sentence for them. Those politicians might be afraid of the voters you mentioned, but they're also afraid of the insurance companies with their deep pockets for negative ads. How do you overcome the lobbyists?"

Proudly, Trump said, "You bribe them!"

"What!" said Obama.

Trump was defensive and a little exasperated. "Not literally. Why does everybody take me literally when they know how sloppy I am with rhetoric? You offer to buy them out. The total stock value, the market capitalization or market cap for the whole insurance industry is about $500 to $600 billion. You buy them out with, say, $750 large, and they make a quick up-front killing. Since single-payer systems are about a third less expensive than ours, we'll make our investment back in a few years—five years tops."

Obama was amazed. Trump had just used statistics and used them accurately. Maybe there was hope for this.

"Anything else?"

"Immigration reform and the Dream Act need to get passed. The public supports both, in general, so I'll use the same pressure for these as for the single-payer stuff," said Trump proudly.

"Homelessness?"

"After I talk to you I'm going to talk to my kids. Rich folks have plenty of housing, but I'll get my own company, and any others I can bully into it, to start building housing for low income. It will require a lot of government subsidies, but when my father and others got them years ago they were able to produce a lot of housing. We can do the same if we loosen up the purse strings a little."

"Yes, how are you going to pay for this?" asked Obama.

"Tax the rich. Simple. They're the only ones with money. Those tax breaks I talked about during the campaign would just ruin the economy and cripple every government program. Under Kennedy taxes were dropped, but only to 70 percent for the highest. The public would be wildly enthusiastic."

"Climate change?" asked Michelle.

"You mean global warming. The first thing is to call it by its right name. Republicans intimidated the press so much that they used this *climate change* euphemism. We have to honor our treaties and spend a ton of money on research."

"Abortion?" asked Michelle.

Trump hesitated. The image of Maria just shocked him into silence.

"Abortion . . . *Roe v. Wade*?" she repeated.

He snapped back to reality. "We have to uphold *Roe* and make sure women have access to all the services they need. If the states won't do it, we'll set up federal clinics and I'll make sure it gets done. They didn't want to give you Garland on the Supreme Court? I send them nominees so liberal they'll make Ruth Bader Ginsberg look like Ayn Rand."

"You know, this is quite a bit. Do you think you can get this by the Congress? I couldn't get anything from them once you guys took over, and when you sandbag them with this change of heart they might not roll over like you're predicting."

"But, Mr. President," Trump said earnestly, "I'm white."

Obama and Michelle both were stunned, but Michelle spoke up first. "Are you admitting that opposition to my husband was because of race?"

"Not all of it. There was also religious fanaticism and greed from the One Percent, but enough race was there to tip the balance. On legislation, too. If immigrants all looked like Ivana or Melania, at least in terms of skin color, do you really think there would be any opposition to reform? And that crackpot theory about you being born in Kenya? People would have laughed it off if they weren't so willing to make you a target. Do you ever get the *Village Voice* down here? It's given away in the city for free."

"The city? No, I don't see the *Village Voice*."

Trump apologized, "New Yorkers have a habit of saying 'the city' when they mean New York. Well, the *Voice* had it best a few years ago when they had a headline that read, 'White America Has Lost Its Mind.' But not all white America, because you did get a good number of white votes when you ran. If Hillary did as good as you did, I wouldn't be here."

Michelle asked, "How about you? How do you feel?" As long as he was confessing she thought she would go for broke and ask the potentially embarrassing question.

"There's no reason for you to believe this, considering what I've put you through the last few years, but I wasn't motivated by racism, only opportunism. And, it seemed to work out pretty well until now and until my inauguration surprise."

Obama looked at Michelle, and they both wondered if he was telling the truth, even now.

"Well, I've got to get over to my family before it gets too late. All this stuff I told you is top secret. I have to drop this on them like a bomb and hope that the surprise will get them confused enough so that they can't put up a fight. Wish me luck."

"Good luck, and know that we'll do anything we can to help."

Trump said good-bye and walked over to his family. He kissed everyone again before taking his oldest three to the side. "There's been a change in plans," he started. "I have it on very good authority, very good authority, that our international plans are going to cause a lot of problems."

They all looked a little puzzled.

"When I'm in office, it will be hard for anyone to go after me. I'll have too much power, and a lot of immunity that comes with the presidency. But, they'll be able to go after you three. If anything happens to any of our deals, or if they just don't like me, as unlikely as that sounds, they will use it as an excuse to go after you."

Donald Junior asked, "So are we supposed to stop building, stop deals?"

"No, but you may have to switch to other ones. Keep building in Manhattan, but start looking out to the boroughs. Don't tell anybody this, but I am going to have a major push to get more low-income housing, and more for the homeless. Dad made a fortune when the subsidies were around and I intend to bring them back, but much, much larger ones. When I'm done, there won't be any homeless shanties left in this country."

Eric spoke next. "But wouldn't that cause conflicts of interest? You're producing subsidies and we're doing business using them?"

"Your grandfather, may he, uh, rest in peace, more or less was able to do business and make money and he survived lots of investigations. These government programs have tons of rules and if you're really, really careful you can stay within them. I'll make sure you have the best people to help you. There's a lot more land in Brooklyn, Queens, and the Bronx than in Manhattan."

Ivanka was shocked. "I'm not going to the Bronx, I don't care how much land is there."

Trump persisted. "There are lots and lots of old brownstones that could be fixed up, the real estate is dirt cheap, and there's good access to subways into the city. We've been trying to gentrify the Bronx for years. There's also a lot of old industrial areas that could make for a large Trump City type development. Don't worry, you won't go broke and have to be on food stamps any time soon."

Ivanka persisted, "You want us to build housing for people who ride the subway? Are you feeling okay, dad? Oh, and I think food stamps are called SNAP now."

It was the one time Trump didn't feel bad about having his words repeated to him.

Donald Junior was still shaking his head. "I just don't see how this is easier than casinos overseas."

"I didn't say it would be easier. But have you seen how many homeless are around the country, and here in the city, and even panhandling on Fifth Avenue? We should be building housing here, not casinos for our enemies like Cuba, Russia, and George Soros."

Ivanka picked up quickly on what he said. "Did you just use *should* as in a moral imperative?"

"Yes, a moral imperative. And it's about time, too. We're not just another rich family in the top one percent. For four years we're going to be the first family of the country. If that doesn't require at least a little morality, then I don't know what will."

The children were quiet for a few seconds; then Eric asked, "How big will these subsidies be?"

"They'll be huge, huge, believe me," Trump said, mimicking himself. They all got the joke and laughed.

"Okay, maybe for a few years we can do this," said Ivanka, as everyone else nodded.

Trump was pleased. Maybe he had just put them on a path that would prevent a midnight visit by their grandfather, or even by him, some future Christmas Eve.

Inauguration day was on a Friday. There were massive crowds, both supporters and opponents, all over Washington, and even spread out throughout the country. Fifth Avenue in New York was completely blocked by demonstrators. But all the crowds grew silent as Trump started to speak.

"I had a dream. It was not as noble as the dream of the great Martin Luther King, Junior, but it was important for our nation and for this time in our history. It was a dream that taught me that the economic inequality that separates the ninety-nine percent from the one percent is immoral, harmful to our nation, and must be reversed after damaging this country for thirty-five years. I pledge to do this with every ounce of strength I have."

Most inaugural speeches are more vague and rhetorical than concrete. But his wasn't. He hit his opponents, the other Republicans, not the Democrats, with a list of every program he intended to implement. He went through single-payer healthcare, immigration reform, housing and homelessness, and many others. When he got to reproductive rights and stated that every woman was entitled to a safe abortion, his voice broke, and the crowd in Washington actually gasped. The crowd in New York was silent for a second, not believing what it just heard, but then a tremendous cheer went up and the next minute or two of the address was drowned out. Many of his supporters around the country were also cheering.

Not cheering were most of the upper-level Republicans in Congress. A few laughed and thought that the great con man had put another one over on the country. But the more careful listeners realized that he was serious. He had adapted the rhetoric of the Occupy Wall Street movement from several years ago. When he complained about thirty-five years of damage to the country, they understood that he was criticizing President Reagan. President Reagan!

They were overwhelmed by the number of issues he threw at them as well as being overwhelmed the following Monday morning, the date of the Monday Morning Massacre when he replaced almost his entire senior staff with one that was handpicked by Senator Schumer. As far as his Supreme Court nominations a few months later, *fugetaboutit!*

Most of his agenda was passed with the coalition of Democrats, Trumpsters, and a few Tea Party supporters. The inequality he condemned did start to turn around, although slowly. Single-payer healthcare came in, and quality increased as costs dropped. When Juan Junior and Maria Rodriguez finished medical school, he personally attended both their graduations, causing quite a scene. He even reconciled with Fred Junior's branch of the family (that's a story for another day). Homelessness dropped to almost nothing, and his family did well with numerous projects, including Trump City North in the South Bronx. None of his children were ever indicted or had to go onto food stamps, uh, SNAP. Every year, he got together with Melchior in front of his house, and donated a large check to New York City charities.

Many years later he was lying in bed, and when he arose he felt strange. He sat up and was blinded by bright sunlight. But, he wasn't sitting on his bed. He was sitting on his sarcophagus. "Donald J. Trump, President of the United States" in gold adorned the lid. Around the back was a large semicircular wall of beautiful white marble engraved with various quotes from him. For a second he panicked and looked around. There were no chains anywhere.

"Well, son, you made it," said a proud, ghostly Fred Trump.

Trump spun around to face his dad. No chains on him, either.

"Yes, son. Somehow they were taken away. I don't know if it was because I did my time, or because your good record rubbed off on me, but they just disappeared one day."

"It's good to see you, dad, and in such great shape, considering we're both dead. Incidentally, is the Ghost of Christmas Yet to Come around here anywhere? I have to apologize for that crack about banshees."

Fred smiled, "I guess you haven't changed completely. I'm just glad you took my advice and ended up here."

He couldn't resist a little needling, so he answered, "Yes, I took your advice, unlike my brother Fred Junior."

"Stop that!" yelled Fred, but smiling all the time. "Come on, let's go meet him. It's time for a family reunion. The other ghost will have to wait."

"It's okay, we've got plenty of time."

POSTSCRIPT

———————————

Unfortunately, this story is fiction. If you would like more factual information, you can read *The Making of Donald Trump* by David Cay Johnston and *Trump: The Greatest Show on Earth* by Wayne Barrett. They are both great books, believe me.